WALKING
THE
NORTHUMBERLAND DALES

Jennifer Norderhaug
& Barbara Thompson

Published by Sigma Leisure – an imprint of
Sigma Press, Stobart House, Pontyclerc, Penybanc Road, Ammanford, Carmarthenshire SA18 3HP, UK

British Library Cataloguing in Publication Data
A CIP record for this book is available from the British Library.

ISBN: 978-1-85058-838-2

Typesetting and Design by: Sigma Press, Ammanford, Carmarthenshire

Cover photographs: (clockwise from top) The Old Boathouse near Thockrington; Rowley Burn near Westburnhope; Tumulus by Riddlehamhope.

Photographs: Ian Barnes and Bill Cresswell

Maps: the authors

Printed by: Bell & Bain Ltd, Glasgow.

Disclaimer: the information in this book is given in good faith and is believed to be correct at the time of publication. No responsibility is accepted by either the authors or publisher for errors or omissions, or for any loss or injury howsoever caused. Only you can judge your own fitness, competence and experience. Do not rely solely on sketch maps for navigation: we strongly recommend the use of appropriate Ordnance Survey (or equivalent) maps.

Preface

Since 1990, many hours have been spent with OS maps devising these walks for groups of adults participating in the local community education programme. The 'Country Walks' course still runs, gaining in popularity year on year as more people become eager to keep fit in some of the most stunning scenery in England. How lucky we are to have it all to enjoy.

However, a traveller without knowledge is like a bird without wings and, as we only observe what we know, the notes accompanying the walks will help you to gain the most pleasure from your outings. A further reading list to increase your knowledge of Northumberland is also given. We are greatly indebted to these authors for increasing our knowledge over the years.

The walks are intended as half-day or evening outings, perhaps using local establishments for refreshments or with a picnic. All are of medium grade and all include some steep hills and stiles. Some are over rough terrain at high altitudes for our country, and serious attention must be paid to safety. We have included some helpful hints on weather, clothing and general conduct in open country and it is sensible to take with you the relevant OS map. Respect the Country Code and Open Access restrictions and take heed of your safety and that of others.

Routes suitable for dogs, with no difficult stiles, are indicated with a clear symbol. While acknowledging the pleasure of including the family dog on walks, the importance of keeping the dog on a lead and away from farm stock cannot be over-emphasised. This is for everyone's well-being and safety, including your own.

Our most heartfelt thanks go to Ian Barnes and Bill Cresswell for their unstinting endeavour to produce an excellent range of photographs. We would also like to thank Ian Thompson and members of the walking groups for their contributions.

These walks have already brought much pleasure to a lot of people. It is hoped that the beauty of south-west Northumberland will now be shared with a wider audience. Enjoy your walking. Enjoy Northumberland. You are most welcome.

Jennifer Norderhaug & Barbara Thompson

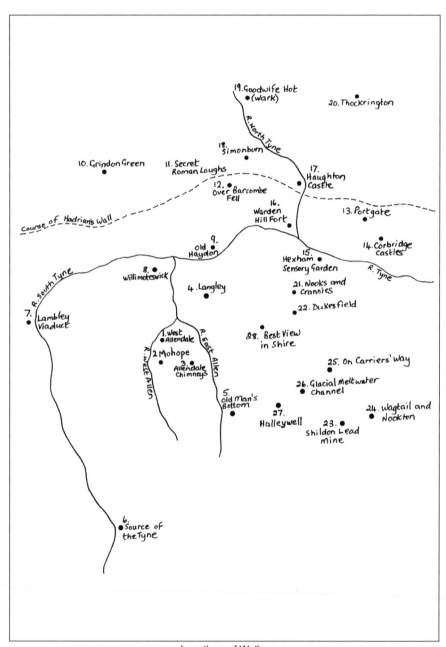

Locations of Walks

Contents

Hexhamshire and Blanchland

Northumberland

Land of far horizons and secret corners

This is still the last county in England where it is possible to walk all day and have for company only the sigh of the wind, the call of the curlew and the ever-changing stunning vistas. Not a soul to disturb the day except, perhaps, for the distant sight of a farmer going quietly about his work, also enjoying his solitude. Peace, a rare tonic and treat in our frenetic world. Northumberland still has its values right.

At 112km long (ten percent of the length of Britain), seventy one percent of Northumberland is still held in large estates owned by private families. This is the highest proportion of private land ownership in the country, a living remnant of our feudal traditions.

The south-west corner of the county forms the backdrop for this book of walks, some of which are in the Northumberland National Park and some in the Area of Outstanding Natural Beauty. The countryside covered includes North and South Tynedale, East and West Allendale, Hexhamshire and Hadrian's Wall country.

One third of the county, mainly the western uplands, is covered by moorland – over five thousand square kilometres of heather moorland, blanket and raised bogs, most of which is managed for red grouse. These moors form some of the most important grouse habitat in the country. This really is the 'black land and white' of the Hexham poet Wilfred W. Gibson – the 'black land' being heather-covered, while the 'white land' owes its colour to the upland bent grass.

Northumberland is England's coldest county; the deepest and longest-lying snow cover is in the part of the county within the North Pennines. In the words of David Bellamy it is 'England's last wilderness'.

In the eighteenth and nineteenth centuries, lead miners cultivated land for smallholdings on the moorland edges of this area up to an exceptional 400m. Much of our industrial lead-mining heritage is clearly visible on the routes of some of these walks. Stones in local churchyards reveal the reality of the times. Some of the highest roads in England meander through the hills here at 600-630m. Although partially in County Durham, Killhope Law, the highest point in south-west Northumberland, towers over the Allen Valleys at 673m.

Waders such as curlew, lapwing, snipe and redshank all add to the springtime pleasure of North Pennine walking. Add to this the chance of sighting ring ouzel, merlin, golden plover, peregrine falcon, red grouse and black grouse at the lek (mating ground) and you begin to understand the special privileges awaiting you in this quiet corner of the county.

Leaving the high ground, this book also shows softer valley, woodland and riverside walks in the beautiful scenery of Tynedale and Hexhamshire. Here you will find the rare Northumbrian wild daffodil, hay meadows as our forebears knew them, vestiges of the ruthless Border Reiver past, Iron Age settlements and, of course, the newly designated World Heritage Site and Scheduled Monument of Hadrian's Wall. Of this, Wainwright commented, 'Fell walking at its best'. Rather than staying on the popular long-distance Hadrian's Wall Trail, these routes explore some lesser-known corners surrounding the Wall.

Helpful Hints

When walking cross-country, the following may be helpful:

General

❖ Check the local weather forecast before setting out.

❖ Advise of your whereabouts and timings. If remote, leave a note on your car windscreen.

❖ Allow plenty of time and only attempt walks within your capability. Usually two miles per hour is an average speed for lowland walking. Allow one mile per hour for mountain terrain with steep ascents, boggy land etc.

❖ Slow and steady always wins – a steady rhythmic pace will be far less tiring than pushing yourself and having to take rests.

❖ Food should include a drink (hot in winter), quick energy foods (high in sugar) and always take too much.

Comfort and Safety

❖ The safest minimum number in the group is four.

❖ Learn some elementary first aid.

❖ If caught in bad weather – huddle against a wall, boulder, ditch etc to get out of the wind. Put on all your extra clothes. Do not rub your skin to try to warm up or drink alcohol – both take the heat from the body core so reducing the temperature at the vital organs.

❖ Walk in single file, a metre apart, across moorland.

❖ Feet – always try to put the whole foot on the ground especially going uphill and downhill, as this is less wearing on the foot.

Clothes

❖ Socks – a thin pair next to the skin, thicker outside. Carry spares.

❖ Boots – comfortable and waterproof; if the boot starts to hurt, take it off immediately and put a plaster over the sore area before a blister develops.

❖ Sweaters – one thin, one thicker, always of wool.

❖ Jacket – water and windproof, preferably able to breathe (e.g. Gore-Tex). Although expensive, on the day you really need it, it could be a lifesaver.

❖ Hat – a substantial amount of body heat is lost through the head.

❖ Gloves – waterproof.

Navigation

❖ Map and compass – moors soon become featureless. A knowledge of direction finding within the group is essential.

❖ Carry a whistle – distress signal: six blasts repeated every minute.

❖ Stick to rights of way and observe the country code.

❖ Always check the maximum height your route will reach (check contour lines).

Dogs

Many of these walks are suitable for dogs on leads and these are indicated with this symbol: 🐕

Walk 1: West Allendale

Route: Keenley Well, Keenley Fell, Keenleyside Hill, Monk Wood, Ashey Bank, Burnlaw, Keenley Well.

Distance: 8km, 5 miles

High point: 378m

Ascent: 230m

Terrain: fields, woods, and lanes.

Refreshments: The Elk's Head, west of Keenleywell House, where the road joins the A686 Alston to Hexham road.

Map: OS Explorer OL43

Start at the crossroads by Keenleywell House (old Keenley School) grid ref NY799570, where there is some room for car parking on the grass verge. With Keenleywell House behind you, walk straight ahead, south-west, uphill along the road about 1km and take the first turn on your left just before Quarry House.

> You are now walking along a spur of land between east and west Allendale and will pass some old limestone quarry workings on the right (now grassed over).

Just after the quarry workings on the right, pass through a gate to visit some restored communal lime kilns (see photograph and Notes, 1). Return to the road and continue south to a way-marker on the right. Cross the stile and ascend the hill to Keenley Fell West farm. You may need to divert round to the right to avoid marshy land.

> The top of this hill is well worth a view-stop. To the north are Catton Beacons (radio and television masts, but this hill was originally part of an ancient chain of beacon look-outs, where fires were lit to warn of attack). Further north you will see Cheviot on a fine day. To the south-east are the Allendale smelt mill chimneys, and to the north-west is Whitfield hill (the next beacon) and beyond it, Carter Bar.

At the top of the hill pass through a gate and, keeping Keenley Fell West to your left, continue along the farm drive to a road and turn left.

> As you walk along the road, on your right runs the scenic West Allen valley (see Notes, 2).

Restored communal lime kiln

After about 1km turn right at a way-marker signed to Monk Cottage. Follow the grassy track between stone walls downhill to a gateway. Continue to the next gate, go through, and pass a small lime kiln immediately on the right. Continue in the same direction passing through another gate, and follow the stony path until you reach a gate on the right (marked Isaac's Tea Trail). Go through this gate taking the path ahead following the contour of the hill. Continue, keeping the stone wall to your right.

After a few hundred metres you will have a commanding view of the West Allen valley to the left, with the Hexham/Alston road visible on the other side of the valley. To the north-west notice Whitfield Hall, the property of the local land-owning family, and the spire of Holy Trinity Church (see Notes, 3).

Continue along the path, which is carpeted with the tiny white flowers of eyebright in summer, and pass through a gate and on into

Eyebright

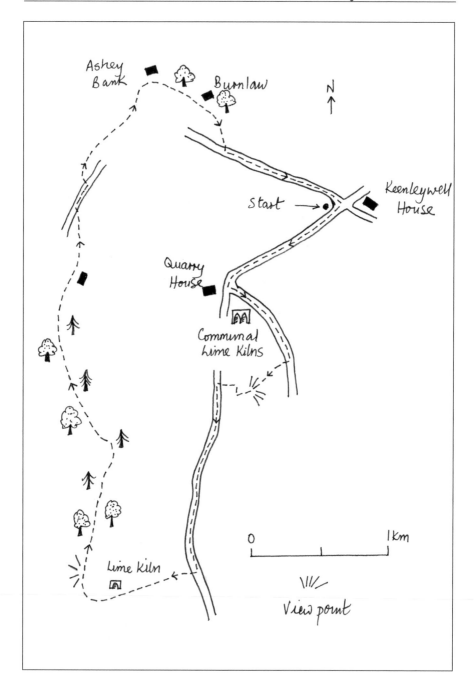

Monk Wood. Notice the pheasant feeders alongside the track. After about 2km, pass through a gate at Monk Farm (see Notes, 4) and follow the track curving to the left.

At the road turn right, and walk about 100m to cross a stile on the left into a field. Walk diagonally right for a short distance to find a trodden path, then continue right on this path keeping parallel to the road. Pass through a gate space in a wall, and on to Harlow Bank. Through the gate, cross the farmyard to another gate on the right of the house and continue in the same direction until you meet the grassy track in front of Asheybank. Take the grassy track to the right keeping the wall to your left. Go through a gate onto a double-walled track and continue uphill past Burnlaw to the road. Turn left and walk along the road to return to Keenleywell House.

Notes

1. In the 18th and 19th centuries each farm would have access to a kiln to make lime for fertilizing the land by neutralising the acidic soil. The limestone would be quarried locally and a kiln built nearby. Some farms would have their own kiln, as you will see later on this walk. Others would share a larger kiln as seen here next to the old quarry workings. The actual kiln or 'pot' is hidden behind the drawing arches. It was filled from the top with alternating layers of limestone and coal, which was then ignited from the 'eye' at the base of the drawing arch. As its name implies, the structure of the arch would help to funnel air into the kiln. The burn would last four to five days at an ideal temperature of 1000°C, after which time the ash and calcium oxide (quick-lime) would be raked out through the eye. The arch structure would afford the lime burner some protection from the weather whilst he was collecting the lime. But he had to protect himself from the intense heat above, whilst being most vigilant not to breathe the poisonous carbon monoxide fumes, which formed from carbon dioxide as it rose through the heat of the kiln.

2. The West Allen River rises in the lead-worked hills high above the tiny hamlet of Coalcleugh next to the Cumbrian border. The confluence of the West and East Allen comes at Whitfield, from where the River Allen flows on to eventually join the South Tyne near Haydon Bridge.

   From this road a good view of the table-topped Cross Fell can be seen to the south-west, with Great and Little Dun Fells beyond. Cross Fell is the highest peak in the north Pennines at 2930ft, sometimes referred to as

Fiend's Fell. Great Dun Fell is easily spotted with its radar masts at 2780ft, and its little sister stands at 2761ft.

Cross Fell is said to take its name from the legend that St Augustine erected a cross on the summit to drive the devils away. It is difficult to imagine how any devil would wish to withstand the ferocious Helm Wind, which sweeps over the Pennines with alarming force. Freezing point can be expected on 132 days of the year on Cross Fell, snow on 70 days and rain on 250 days!

3. Views of Whitfield Hall can be gleaned from the wood. The hall was built in the reign of Henry VI, enlarged in the 17th century, and in 1780 sold to William Ord of Fenham as his shooting lodge. In 1785 it was substantially renovated and by the 1850s the hall and estate had been vastly improved by the wealthy Ords. As can be seen by the pheasant feeders in the wood, game shooting is still an important part of life in the Allendales.

Monk Farm is named after its association with the Canons of Hexham. There are traces of ecclesiastical architecture and the remains of a tithe barn. In 1669 the place was known as Westermuncke and was originally a House of Correction where unruly monks were sent from Hexham Priory to repent.

Walk 2: Mohope (Ninebanks)

Route: Black Pool Bridge, Ninebanks old School, St Mark's Church, Bates Hill, Malakoff Bridge, Hesleywell, Appletree Shield Chapel, Mohope Head lead mine, Nether House, Redheugh, Mohope Burn, Malakoff Bridge, Black Pool Bridge.

Distance: 7.5km, 4¾ miles

High point: 338m

Ascent: 187m

Terrain: rough fields, riverside and lanes. 🐕

Refreshments: The Elk's Head, Whitfield.

Map: OS Explorer OL43

The nearest settlement to the start of this walk is Ninebanks in West Allendale, which you reach from Whitfield, sign-posted off the A686. We suggest that you park in this picturesque hamlet, owned by the local landowner, to have a look at the old buildings including the pele tower (see Notes, 1) and then drive on a short distance to the start of the walk.

Drive south from Ninebanks and where the road forks, take the right fork to Mohope and Alston. Cross the bridge and turn sharp left, parking immediately on the verge on the left at grid ref. NY782523.

Walk back over Black Pool Bridge across the River West Allen, and then climb the steps on the right. Continue up the slope and turn right onto the lane. Almost immediately turn left through the metal gates next to the post box in the wall.

> Take a short diversion to see the Old school and then St Mark's Church, built during lead-mining times and still in use today. The churchyard is the resting place of many West Allendale lead miners. Do look for the gravestone beyond the church on the left of Frances Ritson and her children.

Return to the road and continue ahead. Soon on the left you will pass the old Hearse House, built by Isaac Holden, where the horse-drawn

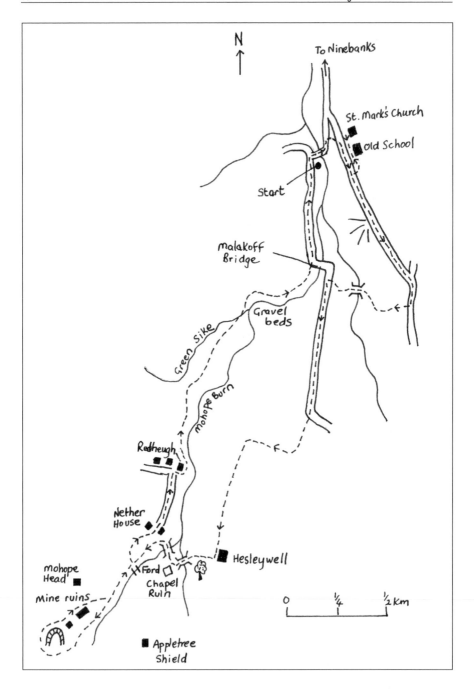

hearse would have been kept. On the right is the old Rectory and walk on to where the view opens out on the right.

Slightly to your left in the valley is the sloping Malakoff Bridge. It is locally believed that returning from the Crimean War, the builder of the bridge gave it the name of the famous battle.

Continue up the lane and pass a lime kiln on the left. For more information on lime kilns see Walk 1. Pass the next house on the right, Bates Hill, and then take the stile to the right, way-marked to Malakoff Bridge. Walk down the steep bank, keeping close to the left side of the ravine. Cross the stone slabs over the ravine and continue down to a wall stile by a bridge to your right. Cross the bridge over the West Allen River and then cross a stile. Follow the fence on the left, uphill, then bear slightly to the right and walk in the direction of the farm ahead. Cross a stile, and notice the Malakoff Bridge to your right, close to the confluence of the River West Allen and Mohope Burn. Turn left and follow the lane for about half a kilometre. Where the lane curves to the left, go through the gate on your right onto Hesleywell Farm lane.

In 1660 Thomas Williamston and his son were put in Morpeth Jail for ten years for holding Quaker meetings here.

This lane curves right and then left, and then you go through a gate. From here your view ahead is of the remains of Wellhope and Mohope Head mine works (see Notes, 2).

At the farm go through the gate and bear left, then right again. Go through the gate ahead and go down the steps.

Take time to look around the valley here. The house to your far left is Appletree Shield House, once the home of various lead-mining families. It was a huge house and even had a ballroom!

Walk down towards Nether House ahead on the other side of the valley following the wall and then fence to your right and then go through a gate in the fence to the steps as the bank falls steeply down.

Ahead of you are all the lead-worked hills. Around where you are walking, look out for red squirrels, as they are often seen in this area.

Continue down the bank and cross the footbridge over Appletree Shield Burn.

Ahead of you now are the ruins of Appletree Shield Chapel, deserted
since the closure of the mines.

Turn right in front of the Chapel and cross the footbridge over
Mohope Burn. At this point it is well worth making a diversion from
the footpath to visit the ruins of Mohope Head Lead Mine. Follow the
fence on your left, passing a gate which leads to a ford on the left. Continue ahead with the river on your left. Go through a gate and walk up
to investigate the ruins (see Notes, 3).

Conditions permitting, you can cross the burn to the level entrance
and then walk back behind the blacksmith's shop. Then walk down
and return to the outward path. Re-trace your steps as far as the gate
leading to the ford, then turn sharp left and walk up the sunken stony
track. At the top, follow the lane as it curves to the right and then left,
and past Nether House. Continue along the lane and go through a gate
before passing the old Mohope Chapel on the left, now converted into
a house. Walk on and through another gate. Where the lane curves to
the left, turn right at Redheugh, following the way-marker to Malakoff
Bridge.

Redheugh was the birthplace of Isaac Holden, mentioned previously, and
the inspiration for Isaac's Tea Trail – a well-known walking route in the
area.

Follow the path to the left in front of the house and go over a wall stile
just past the house. Walk straight ahead through a gap in the wall,
with Mohope Burn on your right and Green Syke on your left, notic-
ing all the lead miners' cottages to the left (see Notes, 4). Continue in
the same direction, going through two more gates. Then gently bear to
the right towards a copse of trees ahead.

On the left notice the spoil heap and capped mine shafts – more
remains of a disused mine.

Make your way towards the gravel bed, keeping Green Sike (stream)
on your left. Where the Sike narrows, cross over and walk along just
before the confluence of the two burns.

The gravel beds here are a good breeding ground for oystercatchers
although the water is still quite heavily contaminated with lead. Look
out for metallophytes (see Notes, 5).

Follow the path and make your way towards Malakoff Bridge. At the left side of the bridge go through a gate and turn left onto the lane. Follow the lane back to your starting point by Black Pool Bridge.

Notes

1. The tiny hamlet of Ninebanks has hardly changed in centuries. In the surrounding area only the ruined miners' cottages, churches and chapels and long overgrown green roads serve as a reminder of the intense activity which lead mining brought to the area until a hundred years ago. Many miners walked miles to work on a Monday morning, and lodged all week in accommodation known as a mine shop. There were more deaths from contagious illnesses passed on in the mine shop, with ten or twelve men sleeping head to toe, than in the mines.

   The pele tower here in Ninebanks, typical of Northumbrian peles, was built in the 14th century as a fortified means of defending a family against attack by the Border Reivers. These skirmishes were common during the next few hundred years and went on in both directions across the border between the feuding families.

2. All the houses that you see in the area were miners' cottages until about a hundred years ago. Many of the miners had small-holdings with a few sheep, pigs or hens to help to eke out their meagre earnings in the mines

Pele Tower at Ninebanks

or smelt mills. Their cottages were rented from the mine owners, who let small acreages to them for this purpose. The company also endeavoured to care for the community's social and spiritual well-being by building chapels and schools. By 1842 the minimum age for boys to enter the mines was ten, before which age they were given schooling to read and write. A ten-year-old would earn sevenpence (3p) a day. Mohope Head mine closed in 1894.

3. First you come to the washing bays on your right, where the lead ore was sorted. Next is the blacksmith's shop. These structures are thought to date from 1743 and the washing bays are now listed as buildings at risk. By the end of the 18th century the blacksmith was being paid ten shillings and sixpence (52p) a week. After the blacksmith's shop, make your way along the wet bank on the left until the little arched entrance to a mine level comes into view on the other side of the burn. It is hard to imagine that miners had to enter through this arch, pouring in water and cramped as it is. Mohope Head mine closed in 1894.

Often in the dark, damp conditions around many of these abandoned entrances or levels grow hard shield fern and hart's tongue fern.

4. The present Youth Hostel was the Mine Manager's house and the mine shop, where the miners slept from Monday to Friday, was next door, and the smithy next to that. The long terrace is Keirsleywell Row where the 1841 census shows 27 men and 24 women living. The Keirsleywell Mine ran from the 16th century to 1872. Just past the YHA was the only inn, called the Green, probably doing well on Fridays and pay-days!

5. These waters are still heavily contaminated with lead and other toxic minerals. Consequently, only metal-tolerant plants can colonise the shingle beaches. These plants are known as metallophytes, and include a specially adapted variety of thrift, alpine penny-cress and mountain pansy. Just how these plants are adapted to be metal-tolerant is not fully understood. One theory is that fungi, growing in association with the roots of the plants, are able to filter out some of the contaminants. The gravel beds of West Allendale are listed as Sites of Special Scientific Interest.

Mountain pansy

Walk 3: Allendale Chimneys

Route: Frolar Meadows, Carriers Way, Allendale chimneys, Dryburn Moor, Hawksteel, Frolar Meadows.

Distance: 8km, 5 miles

High point: 476m

Ascent: 206m

Terrain: Moorland, country lanes. 🐕

Refreshments: There are various pubs and cafes in Allendale

Map: OS Explorer OL43

The walk begins about 2km south-west of Allendale, which you can reach by taking the Ninebanks road from Catton or Allendale. Begin at the three-way cross-road to the west of Frolar Meadows at grid ref. NY817552. There is room for parking on the grass verges. From the beginning, one of the Allendale chimneys is visible to the south-west, so begin by walking along the road in that direction to a gate at the entrance to the moor. Close by is Fell house. From this point onwards you will be on Open Access land. Having gone through the gate, two horizontal flues are visible, one on either side of you, leading to the chimneys. You should take the path which follows along the flue to the right (see Notes, 1).

> You are now on part of an old Carriers Way, along which trains of ponies carried lead. For more information on transport and the lead industry see Walk 25).

After gently ascending for about half a kilometre it is worth turning round to admire the view.

> On a really clear day you will be able to see as far as Cheviot in the north and Carter Bar to the left. Facing north, you are looking down into the Staward gorge in the middle distance, and beyond that, to the Roman Wall. Slightly to the left of the track, in the middle distance, is the Langley smelt mill chimney and in the near distance you can see Catton, Allendale and the East Allen Valley.

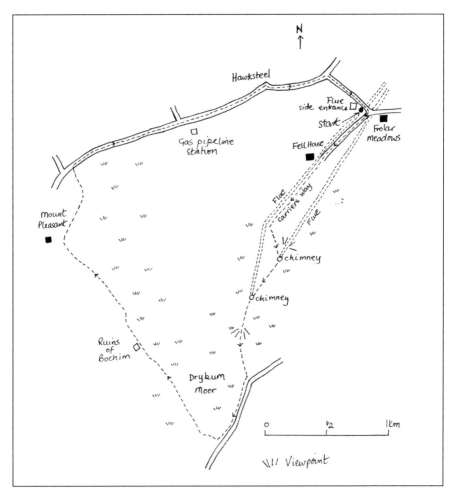

Just before you draw level with the first chimney on the left, divert to visit it by following one of the many sheep tracks – sheep always find the driest routes! From the top you can see the course of the collapsed flue to this chimney.

To the left of the flues you may notice a white post with a red top. This marks the position of the gas pipe-line from Scotland to Teeside. Beyond this in the distance you can make out the light sandstone and two dark arches of a communal lime kiln. For more information on lime kilns, see Walk 1.

Walk on to the next chimney and go inside, where you can see remains of lead deposited on the stones.

This chimney was repaired in the 1980s after being struck by lightening. But it was not restored to its former height. On the outer wall, some of the facing stones have not been replaced, to give an idea of the chimney structure.

Continue straight on following the peaty track up to the fence at the road.

Ahead on a clear day you will have an excellent view of Cross Fell (2947ft) and Great and Little Dun Fells (see Notes, 2).

Allendale chimney and flue

Do not go onto the road, but turn right and walk along the moor, next to the fence.

At the next way-marker (to Public Bridleway) turn right and walk down to the first marker post (see Notes, 3). Continue to descend the fell, following the marker posts all the way down. Part way down, there is a gate on the left and a small ruined house (see Notes, 4). Continue on the path and pass through a gate, which leads onto a double-walled track. Continue through a makeshift gate and then another gate and follow the track up to the next gate, which leads onto a country road. Turn right and walk up the hill past the hamlet of Hawksteel. Take the first turn on the right. Just before you get back to the starting point you will see a restored entrance to the flue.

The margins of this road are well known for localised patches of globe flower and twayblade orchid. Globe flower is a member of the buttercup

family, which stands one to two
metres high, with pale yellow
globe-shaped flowers about two
centimetres across. Twayblade is an
unobtrusive green colour but can be
about half a metre high, with typical
orchid flower spike.

Notes

1. In the notes to accompany walk 4 you
will find more information about smelt
mill flues and chimneys. These extensive flues carried the toxic fumes away
from the smelt mill in Allendale.
Although parts of the flues are now
collapsed, it is still possible to see their
structure. There were several side
entrances to each flue to allow access
for the boys whose job it was to scrape
the precious deposits of lead off the
flue walls.

Globe flower

2. Great Dun Fell can expect fog on two days out of three. It has also experienced the strongest wind in England, 133mph, in 1993, and snow will lie
on Great Dun Fell for at least a hundred days a year!

3. The moors around you are rich in bird life, so be on the lookout for snipe,
curlew, lapwing, black grouse and golden plover. All these birds nest
here, so in spring time, care must be taken to avoid stepping on the eggs in
nests on the ground. It is usually quite obvious if you are near nests as the
parent birds are very protective!

4. These ruins are all that remain of the home of Francis Swindle (or
Swindale), born 1777 of Dryburn, who worked as a supervisor in the lead
industry. He wanted to be a preacher, and having failed to be accepted for
Methodist training, he established his own congregation, supported by
the brother of his second wife, John Clark. This religious group, who
called themselves the Bochimites (this is a Biblical reference found in
Judges 2: 1-5), provided Swindle with this small home and called it
Bochim. This remote cottage became their regular meeting place, where,
it was said, Swindle's sermons consisted mainly of violent tirades against
Wesleyanism.

Walk 4: Langley

Route: Langley, Harsondale, Sillywrea, Lough Green, East Deanraw, Langley.

Distance: 8km, 5 miles

High point: 254m

Ascent: 140m

Terrain: farmland, country lanes. 🐕

Refreshments: Cart's Bog Inn, south-west of Langley, close to where the B6305 meets the A686.

Map: OS Explorer OL43

The walk begins in the centre of Langley on the B6395. Park on one of the verges, as close as possible to the post box at grid ref. NY828611. From the post box, walk west up the little lane alongside the house, which used to be the old shop.

On one of the corner stones can still be seen the 'For Hire' sign for the village taxi. The house to the left, above you, was the home of Catherine Cookson.

At the T-junction turn right and walk to the top of the lane, passing the retaining wall of the fire-clay factory. Some of the old sinks and bricks can be seen in the wall. You turn left onto the barely recognisable disused Hexham/Catton railway line. To your right, in the trees beyond the wooden station buildings, are the crumbling remains of Langley Smelt Mill, which you may consider exploring at the end of the walk (see Notes, 1).

Close to where the buildings end, cross a stile on the right and walk along the field, keeping the wall to your left. Go through the gate and turn left onto the road. Where the road forks, bear right, following the sign to Plankey Mill.

On the left you pass the old school and the high, square water tower (see Notes, 2). As you walk along the lane you have views on the horizon

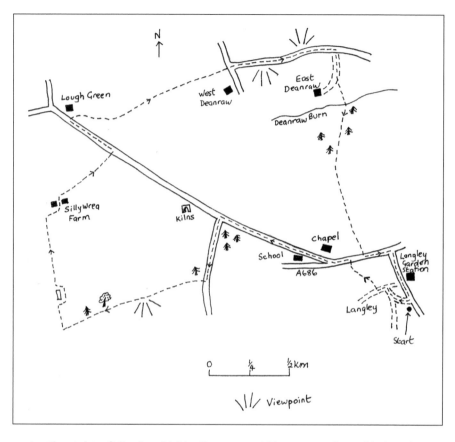

to the right of Sewingshields Craggs and Housesteads on Hadrian's
Wall.

Just past the plantation, take the lane on the left and walk to the end of
the trees on the right. Turn right across a cattle grid and walk along
Harsondale Farm track for about 1km, with views to the left of Catton
Beacons. Cross another cattle grid and walk past a mixed plantation
and then a field on the right. Just before the farm cross the stile on the
right and walk up the edge of the field with the wall on your left. At
the top, cross a stone stile and turn right to another stile and turn left.
This little diversion takes you around the ruins of what was once a
shepherd's thatched cottage and on to two more stiles. From here you
have a view of Sillywrea farm (see Notes, 3).

Looking right you will
see two kilns. These
were part of the
original kilns for the
Fire Clay Factory. The
cottages beside them
were the factory
offices.

Walk down towards the
farm with the wall close
to your left. Skirt to the
right, behind the farm
buildings, and cross the
stile to go through the
farm yard. Turn right,
then continue along the
farm drive for about
half a kilometre and
turn left at the lane.

Clydesdale horse at Sillywrea farm

After another half kilometre turn right at Lough Green and go through
the gate to the right of the house sign. Walk along the straight grassy
track for about half a kilometre passing through two gates, and
continue until you reach the end of a field with two adjacent gates. Go
through the one on the right and continue through another gate until
you reach the cross-road. Here, walk straight on, with a view of
Langley Smelt Mill chimney in the distance to your right.

As the road descends, you will have a view of Haydon Bridge in the valley
ahead.

Turn right at the way-marker to East Deanraw and Langley. At the
farm entrance, cross the cattle grid and take the designated path to the
left keeping close to the fence on your left. Cross Deanraw Burn and
go through the gate following the way-marker arrows. Ascend the hill
towards the stile in the top left of the field. Turn left onto the farm
track and climb the hill with the plantation on your left. Go through
the gate and continue ahead, this time with the plantation on your
right. Continue on the grassy track, which bears diagonally left after a

short distance. At the far side of the field, go through a gate and continue straight ahead to cross a stile. Go down the steps to the road and turn left. After about a quarter of a kilometre turn right at the sign post to Langley and walk back to the starting point.

Notes

1. Langley Smelt Mill was built in 1768 to process the lead mined extensively in the surrounding district. Nearby is a large lake that supplied the power for driving the furnace bellows. The smelting process produced fumes that were known to be harmful to the workers, and they also killed vegetation and livestock. A high wall was built in an attempt to contain the fumes, but this was unsuccessful. So in 1802 an arched horizontal flue was built, partly underground, to carry the fumes away from the population. This flue was extended several times in various directions until the chimney of 1859 was built at the termination of the flue, up on the hill about a mile away. This chimney was restored in 1986 and can be visited from the B6305 Allendale to Hexham road, east of Langley. For more information on the cleaning of smelt mill flues, see Walk 3.

   The road on which you are standing follows the path of the now dismantled Hexham/Catton railway, and if you look back to your right you can see where the railway bridge crossed the road to the station, which still survives. The wooden station buildings now house The Garden Station, open to the public as a centre for gardening and art and craft courses, and well worth a visit.

2. After the two Earls of Derwentwater were beheaded in 1716 and 1746 for the part they played in the Jacobite Rebellion, the Derwentwater lands were put in the charge of the Greenwich Hospital Commissioners, who were in turn responsible for the building of several schools and churches in the area, including this little school at Langley.

3. Sillywrea Farm is one of very few that survive by farming totally traditionally with horses. At the right time of year you may be lucky enough to see a pair of these hardy Clydesdales being used to pull the plough. The name Sillywrea means happy corner.

Walk 5: Old Man's Bottom (Sinderhope)

Route: Sparty Lea, Sipton Bridge, Sipton Cleugh, Sipton Side, Old Man's Bottom, Sipton Plantation, Sipton Terrace, Sparty Lea Bridge, Sparty Lea.

Distance: 7km, 4½ miles

High point: 425m

Ascent: 204m

Terrain: moorland, woodland, riverside, meadow, country road, and one steep climb.

Refreshments: Various inns and tea rooms in Allendale town.

Map: OS Explorer OL43

Some of this walk is over Open Access land where there may be grouse shooting, so it is worth checking with the Open Access Contact Centre before setting off (Telephone 0845 1003298, or email: openaccess@countryside.gov.uk). Park at Sparty Lea, 6 miles south of Allendale on the B6295 at grid ref NY850490. There is plenty of verge space for parking so please avoid blocking any local access.

From the junction at Sparty Lea walk carefully north along the main road for about 1km to Sipton Bridge (see Notes, 1). Cross the bridge and go through the gate on the right. Follow the rough track that winds its way steeply up Sipton Cleugh.

A Cleugh is a deep ravine, though this one is only visible at the beginning of the track.

Eventually, near the top the track bears left and follows the contour of the hillside – Sipton Side – winding through the heather.

This track is used by the ponies from Sinderhope Riding School. The views behind you up the East Allen Valley over Sparty Lea are stunning, and the heather in bloom in July/August makes this walk even more special. Ahead of you on a clear day you will be able to see Cheviot in the far distance.

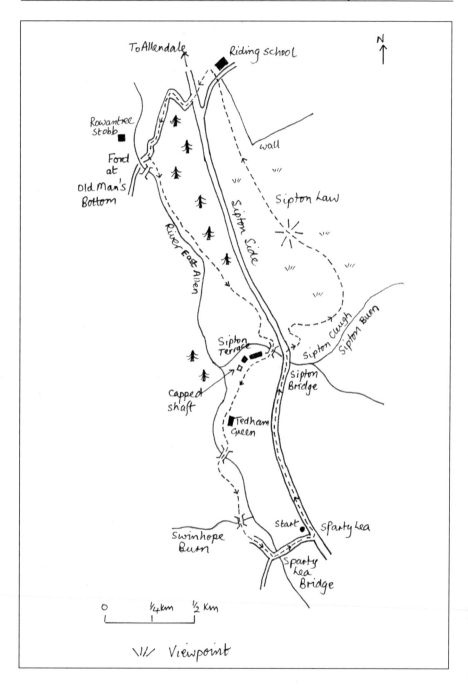

N ↑

To Allendale

Riding school

Rowantree Stobb

Ford at Old Man's Bottom

wall

River East Allen

Sipton Side

Sipton Law

Sipton Clough

Sipton Burn

Sipton Terrace

Capped shaft

Sipton Bridge

Tedham Green

Swinhope Burn

Start

Sparty Lea

Sparty Lea Bridge

0   ¼km   ½ Km

\\⁄⁄ Viewpoint

Slowing the speed of the East Allen River

The track makes its way towards a wall to your right and continues more or less parallel to the wall all the way down to a gate. Go through the gate and cross the grassy patch before you. Then pick up another track bearing left to reach the main road. Cross the road carefully and take the lane opposite descending steeply to the River East Allen at Old Man's Bottom.

> This name does not appear on the map but is well known locally. The lead miners of olden days were known collectively as The Old Man. From here notice ahead over the river the ruined bastle house of Rowantree Stobb.

Just before the bridge and ford, go over the stile on the left, way-marked to Sipton Shield. Take the footpath through the trees keeping the river on your right.

> Please note that the River Allen at this point can be extremely fast and dangerous. Never attempt to cross this ford on foot or by car when in flood (see Notes, 2).

Cross the next stile and turn left to follow the riverbank to another two stiles. Walk alongside the river to some steps cut into the hill on your left. Go up the steps, over the stile and follow the track to cross another stile. Cross the sloping field holding your southerly direction and not losing height. You will pass a bungalow to your right before reaching their driveway. Turn left up the drive, through their gate and follow the stony track to where it forks. Take the right hand fork and follow the path over a small bridge, looking from here to your left to see the underside of the listed Sipton Bridge.

Continue to the metalled lane, turn right and walk past the row of former lead miners' cottages known as Sipton Terrace on your right. All the buildings in this area were part of the lead mining industry (see Notes, 3).

Follow the lane to the riverside, past Tedham Green cottages on your left. Over the bridge turn left, then go over the stile on the right. Turn left and, keeping the fence on your left, walk through two fields and a gate to a stile on the left.

> These are lovely old-fashioned hay meadows in the summer. The semi-parasitic Yellow Rattle is common in this area.

Yellow Rattle

Go over the stile and turn right to follow the river to the metalled lane. Walk on, crossing the bridge over the Swinhope Burn before reaching the next lane at Sparty Lea Bridge. Cross the bridge and walk uphill to return to the start.

Notes

1. Sipton Bridge is a listed Bridge, being one of very few double arched bridges remaining.
2. It is the speed of the Pennine rivers that makes them so precarious due to the high and large catchment area. Only the Findhorn and the Spey in Scotland have been known to rival the speed of the Pennine rivers in

flood. Notice the stoppers placed in the river here and later to slow down the flow.

3. Sipton Terrace is a typical row of lead miners' cottages. The next detached ruined house that you reach was the Mine Manager's house. The small barn over the field to the left was the gunpowder house, kept a distance away for obvious reasons. Notice the capped Sipton Head mineshaft on your right. Access to the mine was by ladder from the top. There was a waterwheel here, almost the size of the restored Killhope wheel until the 1960s. The workforce in this area was huge. Every cottage you see on this walk would have been inhabited by large lead-mining families only 100 years ago.

Walk 6: Ashgill Force and the Source of the South Tyne

Route: Hill House (3km south of Garrigill), Dorthgill, Cocklake, Calvertfold, source of the South Tyne, watershed, South Tyne Trail, Tynehead, Hill House.

Distance: 7km, 4½ miles

High point: 556m

Ascent: 125m

Terrain: gravelled track, footpath. 🐕

Refreshments: George and Dragon, Garrigill; many pubs in Alston. Teas and snacks at Thortergill Tearooms, Garrigill in summer.

Map: OS Outdoor Leisure 31 Teesdale

This walk takes us just out of Northumberland onto Alston Moor in Cumbria. But we feel fully justified in including it as it takes us to the source of the river that has formed the landscape of so many of the walks in this book. Also, to reach the start of this walk you drive through beautiful wild countryside, dotted with interesting historical remains of the lead industry. The walk is relatively short and not particularly demanding, so we suggest an interesting short walk to combine with this one with a short drive of about 2 miles between the two. Alternatively you could walk the whole distance, making it a 12km (7½ mile) walk.

From the top of the cobbled main street in Alston, drive along the B6277 Barnard Castle road south for four and a half miles to Ashgill Bridge at grid ref NY759405. Park in the lay-by on the north side of the bridge and walk over the bridge to cross a stile on the right. Follow the track downhill taking the first turn to the right. This brings you back, above the riverside, to Ashgill Force waterfall below the bridge. You can then enjoy the unique experience of walking in behind the waterfall for a few minutes. Then re-trace your footsteps back to your car.

For the second part of the walk, turn the car around and drive back

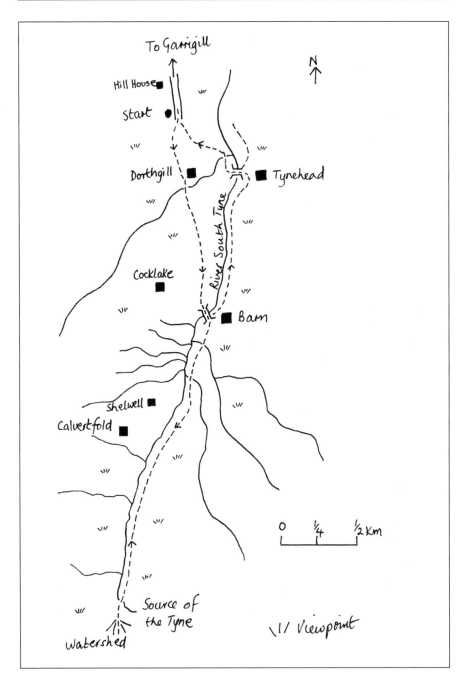

along the road taking the left turn to Garrigill. In Garrigill bear left after the George and Dragon pub and continue until the road runs out at a cattle grid just beyond Hill House. Park here at grid ref NY757383.

Notice, on the hillside opposite, the ski tow on Yad Moss.

Walk across the cattle grid or through the side gate and take the right hand path. Keep to the path, crossing several cattle grids and it will lead you to the source of the Tyne, about 3km away. There are several interesting ruins and landscape features to look out for on the way.

Dotted all over the OS map you will see 'sink holes', or regular hollows in the ground. You will also see many small and larger hills around you as you walk which are spoil heaps from the mining industry (see Notes, 1). The sink holes together with numerous disused mine-shafts make this a dangerous area to roam around. Do not leave the designated path or allow a dog to roam away from the track.

Near the beginning of the track on the left notice the semi-ruined low building with a corrugated roof. This is a sheep shelter (see Notes, 2).

The next house you reach is Dorthgill on the left. There are old mine levels, or side entrances below the house. Across the river in the near distance to the left you can see Tynehead farm (see Notes, 3). The next ruin to be passed is Cocklake on the right, close to where your path crosses the stream, which is the South Tyne.

There was a mine and a smelt mill here in the 18th and 19th centuries.

The area is marked by a modern barn today. Just below this point the waterfall marks the place where the river cuts through the Whin Sill. For more information on the Whin Sill see Walk 20.

The wildlife of the area is interesting and plentiful (see Notes, 4).

As you walk along, you will notice that the hillsides along the way are dotted with the ruined remains of miners' cottages and mine shops (lodging houses where some of the miners and boys spent the week, returning home at the weekends) as well as the actual mine and smelt mill structures. The more obvious of these are Shelwell and then Calvertfold on your right before another mine with predominant spoil heap and track.

Sculpture at the source of the South Tyne

Eventually you will see the stone carving on the left that marks the source of the River South Tyne (see Notes, 5). There are several small streams that feed into the South Tyne, but it has been agreed that the one now marked by the stone is the actual source, and you can trace it right back to the place where it emerges as a spring from the hillside. From here, walk a few more metres along the track to where it levels out and then starts to fall. This is part of the Pennine watershed.

Ahead and slightly right you will have views of Great and Little Dun Fells, covered in fog for up to a hundred days a year! (See notes 6).

Our walk turns back here, although it is possible to continue on to the River Tees and the Moor House Nature Centre. When you turn back, you can either re-trace your footsteps to the starting point, or, follow the river back to the footbridge and then take the right fork to follow the South Tyne Trail. This takes you through more mining country and closer to Tynehead. Walk as far as Dorthgillfoot, then ascend their access track to join the original path at the cattle grid by the start of the walk.

If you decide to take the longer walk from Ashgill Bridge to the starting point of this walk, you will see from your OS map that there is a footpath which will bring you across the valley, alongside the river parallel to the Garrigill road as far upstream as Dorthgillfoot, and then up the track to join the road just north of Hill House.

This walk takes you through some very important and protected hay meadows.

Notes

1. Sink holes, shake holes and swallow holes are commonly found in limestone country. Limestone, being relatively soft, is subjected to constant erosion from rain water, causing fissures in the rock. Sink holes are formed when the top layer of boulder clay collapses into these fissures in the underlying limestone. You will see many such circular depressions measuring a few metres across. Be aware that these holes can be very deep. Most of the rocks underlying Alston Moor are sedimentary limestone, sandstone and shale. As the glaciers of the last ice age moved across these rocks, the irregular erosion resulted in what now can be seen as 'stepping' on the hillsides. This terraced effect can be observed very clearly on some of the hills to your left, near the beginning of the walk. Spoil heaps can be seen all along this walk, and although most of them are the debris from lead mines, a few at the beginning are very black, showing that there must have been some coal mining taking place in the area too.

2. The winters here are long and snowy, so sheep are brought close to the farms and given shelter. You may have noticed the striped poles at the roadsides as you were driving here. These are snow poles, which delineate the roads and provide information as to the depth of the snow by the foot width of the stripes.

   It is thought that Norsemen were the first people to inhabit this area and introduce sheep to the landscape. The hardy Swaledales with black heads, white noses and curly horns are the most commonly found breed in the area today.

3. The farm is all that remains at Tynehead of a thriving hamlet, originally independent of Alston Moor and having its own Lord of the Manor. The Tynehead mine had several levels, or entrances, from different heights on the hillside. Lead ore was transported out of the mine by Galloway ponies, and the miners carried candles to light their way. The ore in this

and the surrounding mines had the
highest silver content in the country,
and the silver was transported from
here to the Royal Mint at Carlisle.

Golden plover

4. In the summer there is a wide variety of
   wild flowers including mountain
   pansies and eyebright, and the quite
   rare sandwort and alpine penny cress
   growing on the disturbed ground of the
   spoil heaps. Grouse, lapwings,
   curlews, golden plover, dippers and
   ring ouzels are all commonly seen in this area.

5. The sculpture marking the source of the River South Tyne was made by
   Gilbert Wood, a local sculptor from Prudhamstone, Fourstones near
   Hexham.

6. The Forestry Commission has experimented with tree planting at different heights, noting average temperatures and wind speeds in different
   locations. The mean wind speed in Britain is 20-30km per hour
   compared with a mean of 37 km per hour and gusts up to 214 km per hour
   on Great Dun Fell. The scientific conclusion was that planting up to
   about 1000m is viable for most of the country, but that because of the
   depressing effect on growth of excessive winds, planting in
   Northumberland is only viable up to 600-700m (Lunn 2004).

Walk 7: Lambley Viaduct

Route: Featherstone, South Tyne Trail, Lambley Viaduct, Diamond Oak, disused prisoner-of-war camp, Hall Bank, Featherstone.

Distance: 7.5km, 4¾ miles

High point: 189m

Ascent: 142m

Terrain: old railway line, riverside, and lane. 🐕

Refreshments: Wallace Arms, a short distance east of the starting point.

Map: OS Explorer OL43

This walk begins on the South Tyne Trail near Featherstone, grid ref. NY681607, where there is substantial parking just to the east of the trail on old railway land. Turn left onto the trail and walk south for about 2 km.

> You are walking along the course of the Alston/Haltwhistle branch line, and the station platforms, stone bridges, cuttings and embankments are all evocative of our Victorian railway heritage (see Notes, 1).

Eventually the view of the river opens up and you approach Lambley Viaduct (see Notes, 2). Cross the viaduct to the far end and descend the steps on the right until you come to a cross-road on the path with a four-way marker. Go straight on, following the sign to Coanwood and footbridge. Go over a stile and then down steps, and turn left along the river bank before crossing the footbridge. Over the river turn left, and continue along the path, then cross a stile, at which point the path widens out onto the flood-plain of the river. Walk diagonally right to cross the flood-plain gradually, moving towards the bank which runs along your right. Soon you will see a marker post on the right at the top of the bank. Climb up here and follow the path straight ahead away from the river.

At the top of the field go through the gate on the left and over the footbridge. After passing a small complex of houses on the left, walk

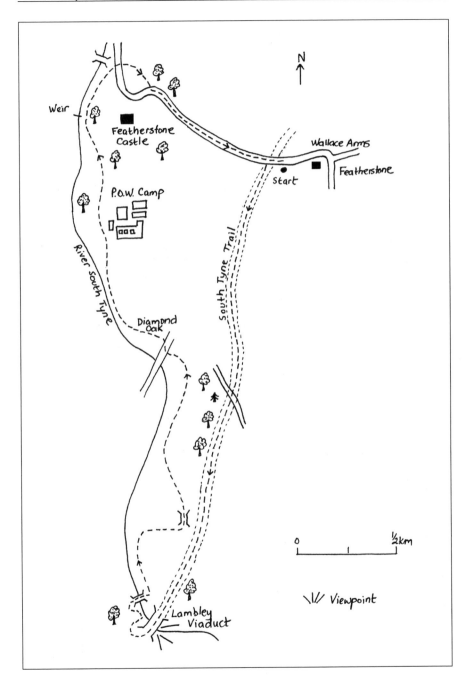

N

Weir

Featherstone
Castle

Wallace Arms

Start

Featherstone

P.O.W. Camp

River South Tyne

South Tyne Trail

Diamond
Oak

0   ½km

Lambley
Viaduct

\|/ Viewpoint

Lambley viaduct

straight on, leaving the stony track, and following the grassy path across the field towards a clump of trees and then on towards the river. This area can be quite wet, but it is possible to skirt around it. Continue along the path, which eventually climbs up to a gate. After going through the gate, turn right and cross the road. Then immediately take the path on the left, way-marked Featherstone, to follow along the riverbank again.

This is an excellent area to see oystercatchers in late spring.

Continue for about 1km, passing through a gate and then eventually coming to the remains of a prisoner-of-war camp (see Notes, 3). Walk through the camp and then out through the remaining gate-posts.

If you turn back at this point you will be able to read the inscription on one of the posts, dedicated to the interpreter of the camp.

From here you will have a good view of the privately owned Featherstone Castle (see Notes, 4). As the track curves right, branch off to the left on the way-marked path and walk along the edge of the river past the weir.

In the autumn, you may see salmon leaping here.

When you are level with the footbridge, go through the gate on the right and cross the road. Cross the stile opposite and then head up the path, but cut diagonally to the right to another stile, which brings you back onto the road.

By doing this, you will have cut a corner off the road, which, alternatively, you could have walked up from the footbridge.

Turn left and continue up the road to return to your starting point.

Notes

1. During the Industrial Revolution, lead, coal and limestone were mined widely in this part of the country. These products were transported by pack-horse until the advent of the railways, when many branch-lines such as this between Alston and Haltwhistle were opened. From Haltwhistle the goods were then transferred to the Newcastle/Carlisle line. Later the line became important for passenger transport too, enabling much greater freedom for travel and communication.

2. Lambley Viaduct was built in 1852. Since the closure of the line it had fallen into disrepair, but it was restored in 1994/96 and is now Grade II listed. At one time a pedestrian footbridge was attached to the viaduct, but a footbridge just north of the viaduct has replaced this. The views from this viaduct are truly spectacular. But whilst looking at the wide landscapes, don't forget to keep an eye open for otters which inhabit this part of the river, and of course the leaping salmon and trout on which they feed. This is also a favourite habitat for oyster catchers, yellow wagtails, grey wagtails, sandpipers and the endangered water voles.

3. As you approach the old prisoner-of-war camp, all you see at first are a few utilitarian brick buildings. But as you move closer it is possible to find the foundations of many more buildings. This was Camp 18, which housed German officers. In its remote setting on the river bank you get an eerie sense of how life must have been here. The plaque on the gate, as you leave, tells of the camp interpreter, who dedicated his time here to promoting British/German reconciliation.

4. Featherstone Castle as it stands today, was mainly constructed in the 19th century, though it has parts dating back to the 13th century, and was greatly renovated in the 18th century. It was the family home of the Featherstonehaughs (a haugh being a meadow or flat land by a river), who later dropped the 'haugh' from their name. The legend of this castle is that the Lord in the 17th century forced his daughter into an arranged marriage, only to find that the wedding party was killed by bandits. The wedding party and their coaches and horses are said to haunt the castle grounds on the anniversary of the wedding.

Walk 8: Willimoteswick

Route: Partridge Nest farm, Willimoteswick, Oadhall Mill, Haughstrother Wood, The Shank, High Barns, Allensgreen, Willimoteswick, Partridge Nest farm.

Distance: 9km, 5½ miles

High point: 206m

Ascent: 186m

Terrain: fields, woodland, and lanes.

Map: OS Explorer OL43

From Haydon Bridge travelling west, take the left turning off the A69 just before Bardon Mill, signed to Ridley Hall and Beltingham. Travelling from Bardon Mill this is the first major turning to the right off the A69. Follow signs to Beltingham, passing through the village and on for about 0.5km. Just before Partridge Nest farm you will reach a parking area on the right side of the road close to a footbridge over the River South Tyne. Park here at grid ref NY780642.

Walk in a westerly direction along the road, passing Partridge Nest farm, and on to Willimoteswick farm to look at the tower (see Notes, 1).

Take the path to the right of the tower and walk down towards the river to Oadhall Mill. At the mill, go straight on through the gate, passing the barn on your right. Cross a stile and continue ahead, passing the lakes of Haltwhistle Angling Club on your right.

At most times of the year these lakes provide a habitat for various wildfowl.

After about 200m take the left fork onto a grassy path which leads up into Haughstrother Woods. Go through a gate, and very quickly the path forks. Take the right fork. Pass through another gate, and out of the woods. Continue along the grassy track with a rabbit-proof fence to your right (see Notes, 2).

Go through the next gate and continue alongside the fence.

The gravel beds along the river here are a favourite haunt of Oystercatchers in the spring when they come here to nest.

After the next gate, turn immediately left and walk up to meet the

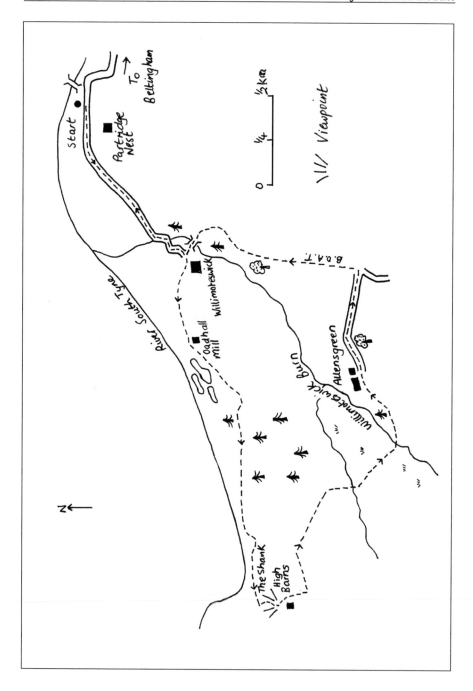

stony path. Follow this path up to High Barns. It is quite steep, so you can stop to admire the view behind you to the north across the South Tyne valley! After High Barns, continue uphill and turn left at the second gate in the wall on the left. Follow the track along the field and through the next gateway. From this point, head uphill diagonally to the right, making for the opposite corner of the field. Go through the gate and walk straight ahead, keeping the wall to your left. Where the wall ends, cross the stream to your left and continue up the path to go through a gateway.

Continue straight for a short distance until you have passed a clump of trees on your left. Then bear right, and go slightly diagonally across the field. The pathway is quite obscure on the ground, although clearly marked on the OS map. Make for the right hand end of the trees ahead, and cross the little burn at stepping stones. Turn left, passing a small waterfall and then go through a gate and continue along the path that edges the plantation on your left. Go through three more gates past a barn and then Allensgreen Farm on your left. After going through the next gate turn right onto the metalled road and continue uphill. The road bends right over a cattle grid, but you should turn left here and go through the gate. The grassy track on which you are now standing is an ancient highway, now designated a BOAT (see Notes, 3). Follow the path gently downwards, passing through four gates, over a foot bridge, then through two more gates at Willimoteswick. Turn right and walk along the road to return to the starting point.

Notes

1. Willimoteswick is now a farm, but was originally the fortified home of the Ridley family. It is reputed to have been the birthplace of the martyr Bishop Ridley, who was burned at the stake outside Baliol College, Oxford in 1555 for heresy. Parts of the house appear to be from as early as the 13th century, but the pele tower-styled gatehouse which stands before us at the north end of the buildings, is more likely to date from about 1600. The walls are about 7ft thick and would have housed the family at times of attack both during border skirmishes and in battles with neighbouring estates. There seem to have been many feuds with neighbours in the troubled history of Willimoteswick Castle, as detailed in Tomlinson's Comprehensive Guide to the County of Northumberland (1999 Newgate Press, first published 1888).

The pele tower at Willimoteswick

2. This rabbit-proof fence is one of the ways that farmers control the number of rabbits attacking their crops. As you walk along, notice the traps which appear at regular intervals at ground level. These are pit traps, which consist of a see-saw trapdoor through which the rabbits fall into a pit beneath. The farmer then comes along regularly and empties the traps. When not activated, a bolt stops the see-saw floor action of the trap.

3. BOAT stands for Byway Open to All Traffic. Over the past decade, the motor cycling fraternity has challenged the designation of footpaths and bridleways in an attempt to open some of them up for motor cycling. If the route can be proven to have been a highway historically (these were officially designated as far back as the 1700s), it must remain a highway today and be open to all pedestrian, mounted and vehicular traffic. There is however a move to repeal the law in order to protect the flora, fauna and peace of our wild areas.

Walk 9: Old Haydon

Route: Chesterwood, Honeycrook Burn, Haresby Road, North Road, New Alston, East and West Haydon, The Tofts, Chesterwood.

Distance: 8.5km, 5¼ miles

High point: 230m

Ascent: 161m

Terrain: farmland, quiet lanes. 🐕

Refreshments: The Anchor, and The General Havelock, both in Haydon Bridge

Map: OS Explorer OL43

The walk begins in the hamlet of Chesterwood, north of Haydon Bridge, grid ref NY830651, where you will be able to find parking space on one of the grass verges.

The collection of houses comprises mainly converted bastles, or fortified houses. At the time of the Border Reivers, the rich protected themselves in their castles or pele towers. Poorer folk made do with a bastle house (see Notes, 1).

Walk west through the middle of the hamlet following the public footpath way-marker. Go through the gate of Park Cottage and, as the track bends left, leave it to follow the way-marker arrows straight on between the houses. Go over a stile and through a gate and walk on with the wall on your right. The path will lead you straight ahead, over three stiles, a footbridge, another stile and another footbridge over the Honeycrook Burn. You will then emerge from the trees onto a metalled lane where you turn right. When you come to the fork, bear right uphill, signed to Whinnetley, and continue for about half a kilometre. Take the next right turn, way-marked to Haresby Road which you will reach after about another kilometre. At the T-junction stop for a few minutes before turning right, and look towards the expanse of land to the north-west.

This is the Muckle Moss — a most important valley bog and an area not

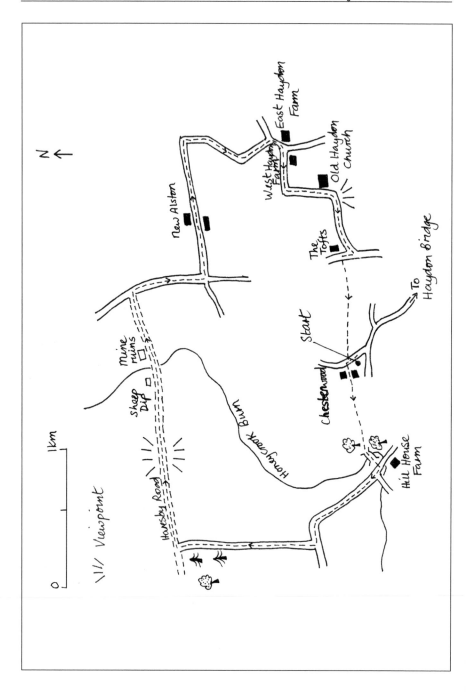

to be walked over. The peat at the centre of the Muckle Moss is about 13m deep. The Moss is 2.5km long and dotted with pools up to 7m deep, often only covered with a thin layer of sphagnum moss. Parts of the Moss have been found to be floating eastwards. Pearson (1960 and 1979) planted canes, which in seven years moved 3.59m (Lunn 2004)

Turn right and walk along this now grassed-over road, passing through two gates.

You will have commanding views on your left to Hadrian's Wall and on your right to the South Tyne Valley and beyond. After the second gate, notice the sheep dip and the remains of lead-mine buildings on the left, close to where the road crosses Honeycrook Burn (see Notes, 2).

At North Road turn right and then at the cross-road turn left, signed to New Alston. After passing through this hamlet, follow the road where it curves through ninety degrees to the right. Continue downhill to where East Haydon Farm and West Haydon Farm are on opposite sides of the road. At this point you should take the right fork to walk west and then south to Haydon Old Church on your left (see Notes, 3).

After visiting the church continue down the road to a viewpoint across the South Tyne Valley with Haydon Bridge below (see Notes, 4). At the T-junction by The Tofts turn right and almost immediately turn left over a stone stile, way-marked to Chesterwood. Walk along next to the wall and then continue more or less straight ahead crossing six short fields with six stiles, to return to your starting point in Chesterwood.

Notes

1. Bastle houses are recognisable by their very large protective corner stones and metre thick walls. A byre door would be the only entrance on the ground floor, giving access to a place of safety for the animals during border raids. An entrance door to the living accommodation would be at first floor level, usually on the south side, and usually with a wooden ladder which could be drawn up for safety. Later, when peace returned to the borders, some built external stone steps up to the first floor and continued to use the ground floor as a byre, thus providing a form of early domestic heating generated by the animals!

This settlement was originally known as Chesterworth meaning 'the enclosure or farm by the camp'.

2. In the 1870s there were Langley Barony lead-mines to the north of Chesterwood. The remains of various buildings can be seen in the narrow valley of the Honeycrook Burn, which rises in the wetlands of Muckle Moss, including the shaft which you pass on the road.

The Honeycrook Burn

3. Haydon Old Church stands on the site of the ancient centre of Haydon. There was even a market at Old Haydon until 1835. The church was built in 1190 with a chantry chapel added in the 14th century. Much of the stone is Roman and thought to have come from Borcovicus. There are many interesting architectural features in the church, in particular a triplet of lancet windows at the east end and a beautiful window from the Decorated period (1315-60). The font was a Roman altar. In the churchyard, still in use, is a strange arch of yews and lying flat a gravestone with a very interesting inscription. Near the church is Cruel Syke – a rivulet thought to be the scene of some ancient fray during which the stream is said to have run with blood.

4. Langley Castle across the valley originated in the 13th century, but was ruined in 1405 by Henry IV during Archbishop Scrope's rebellion. In the 1890s it was restored by Cadwallader Bates. It is now a hotel but still retains many interesting architectural details of eight centuries.

During the industrial revolution Haydon Bridge was a centre of mining and industrial activity, including the Ironworks (established in 1843), two lead mines and the Langley Smelt Mill.

The artist, John Martin was born in Haydon Bridge in 1789. Of humble origin, he gained fame within his own life-time and in 1850 his three famous judgement paintings were valued at £8,000. These atmospheric paintings, depicting God's wrath in scenes of fire and thunder, are known to have been inspired by the vision of smelt mills and furnaces lighting the night sky in his native Tyne valley. The Laing Gallery in Newcastle has a small collection of Martin's paintings.

Walk 10: Grindon Green

Route: The Bent, Tod Sike, Grindon Green, Henshaw Common, Hindleysteel, Hopealone, and The Bent.

Distance: 8km, 5 miles

High point: 299m

Ascent: 119m

Terrain: Plantation, forest drives.

Refreshments: Milecastle Inn and Twice Brewed Inn, both on the Military Road.

Map: OS Explorer OL43

This walk takes place on Forestry land in the Northumberland National Park. From the OS map it looks as if the entire walk is in thick forest, but because of the nature of forestry planting, there are open areas where trees have recently been felled and other areas of new small trees with an open aspect. The walk begins in one of these open areas.

From the Milecastle Inn on the Military Road, B6318, drive east and take the turn-off on the left signed to Edges Green. The walk starts about 3½ miles north of here. Where the road runs out at Scotchcoultard, bear right, and a few metres along the track there is room to park on the right at grid ref. NY726713.

With your back to the car park, turn left and walk back to join the metalled road, where you turn right. Notice the sign to Scotchcoultard (see Notes, 1). At the gate go straight on for about 2km until you reach a ford (Tod Sike). Cross at the footbridge just to the right, where it is worth looking for a heron. You may be lucky. Then continue on the path as it swings to the right.

After another 1km you reach the ghostly remains of Grindon Green, marked only by broken boundary walls and dead trees (see Notes, 2). Continue ahead for a short distance, going past a path way-marked to Hindleysteel on your right, and take the forest road, which is next on

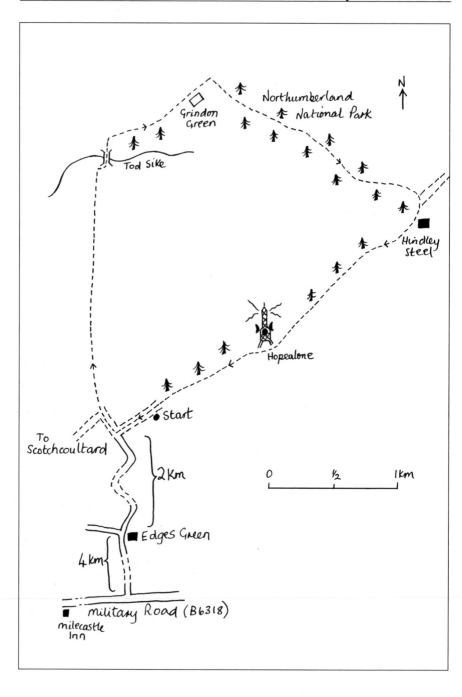

the right. Follow this road through the forest, and where another track joins from the left, continue on your road as it curves round to the right. You will then pass Hindleysteel on your left (see Notes, 3).

After about 1km you will reach Hopealone telecommunications mast (see Notes, 4), and from here the path will bring you back to the starting point.

Notes

1. Many skeletons have been found at Scotchcoultard dating from the 14th/15th centuries, showing it to be a place of battles and skirmishes between the escaping Scottish and Northumbrian Reivers (riders) and the law-keepers of both sides, including the Tynedale Wardens of the English Middle March. These difficult, marshy lands were often the refuge of the worst of the Scottish outlaws, who considered that once they had reached Scotchcoultard on the edge of the 'easy riding', they would make it to the 'debatable lands', their safe haven of Liddesdale. They used their local knowledge to enable them to herd stolen cattle, horses and sheep safely through the treacherous bog land. The Tynedale law-keepers would not chance their horses past this point. From the early

A ghost at Grindon Green?

14th century, for nearly 400 years, the border families of Reivers kept up the battle of raids and thefts across this marshy barrier between England and Scotland. Although the landscape has changed since the introduction of the plantation, it is still easy to stand at this lonely point on a misty day and maybe hear the pounding of horses' hooves!

2. Grindon Green was a thriving farm until the land was taken over for plantation by the Forestry Commission in the 1960s. At this time, the inhabitants were evacuated and re-housed elsewhere. In order to utilise the stone for forest roads, the buildings were almost totally razed to the ground, and now all that remain are a few boundary walls and the gable end of a small building.

3. The derivation of the name Hindleysteel is a ridge or point of land (steel) by a meadow (ley) where hinds (deer) graze. Some of the most important raised and intermediate bogs in Britain are to be found in Northumberland, and one of the largest, at 400 hectares, lay north of Hindleysteel. During the 1950s and 60s the Forestry Commission drained many of the areas in Kielder Forest in order to plant Sitka Spruce and Lodgepole Pine. Happily, they decided to leave the wettest area at Hindleysteel to its own devices – it being too wet to drain- and by 1978, having retained its natural vegetation, this area had become the Grain Heads Moss National Nature Reserve. More recently this is known as a section of the Kielder Mires National Nature Reserve.

4. The Hopealone mast occupies the site of the former Hopealone Farmhouse, one female resident of which used to collect bilberries and walk to Haltwhistle market to sell her wares! The mast was originally erected as part of the early warning system in the 1950s. Now it is a telecommunications station owned by Telecom

Walk 11: Secret Roman Loughs

Route: Old Repeater Station on Military Road, Old School, Sewing Shields, Folly Lake, Halleypike Lough, lime kilns, Sewing Shields, Repeater Station.

Distance: 6km, 3¾ miles

High Point: 265m

Ascent: 116m

Terrain: grassland, rough tracks.

Refreshments: Milecastle Inn and Twice Brewed, six miles and three miles west respectively on the Military Road. Snacks at the Repeater Station in season.

Map: OS Explorer OL43

There is only one path to these loughs (lakes), so you return along the same route, but the vistas are so different in each direction that this does not detract from the enjoyment of the walk. At any time of the year there can be many people walking the well trodden routes along Hadrian's Wall, but this path is seldom taken by walkers, so has a unique atmosphere of remoteness. There are many rare plants in the area including oak fern, moonwort and mountain parsley fern.

Park just off the Military Road by the old Repeater Station (telephone exchange, now a café and accommodation for walkers). This is situated about 3 miles to the north-west of Haydon Bridge along North Road, at Grid ref NY815700.

Walk with care across the Military Road and go through the gate opposite. Turn left and cross the stile onto the permissive path that runs parallel to the road. Walk towards the building on the brow of the hill ahead. This is an old school and cottage. Follow the path around the right side of the old school and turn right onto the farm track ahead.

Soon you will cross the course of the Roman vallum (part of the

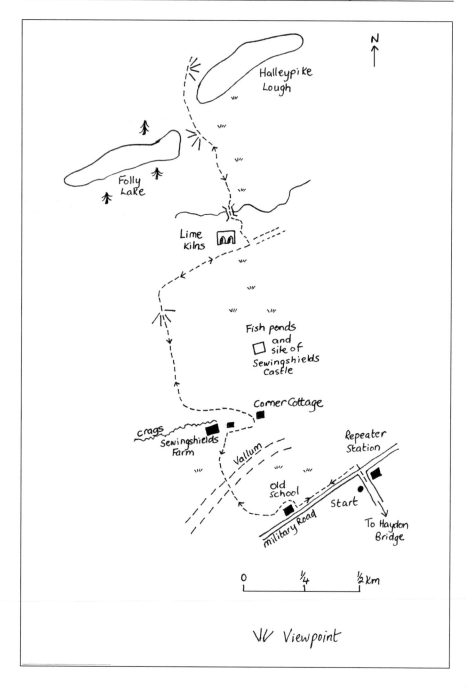

N

Halleypike
Lough

Folly
Lake

Lime
Kilns

Fish ponds
and
site of
Sewingshields
Castle

Corner Cottage

crags

Sewingshields
Farm

Vallum

Repeater
Station

old
school

military Road

Start

To Haydon
Bridge

0   ¼   ½ km

ᾝᾝ Viewpoint

Sheep grazing near Hadrian's Wall

defensive system), which diverts away from Hadrian's Wall at this point where the Wall crosses Sewingshields Crags.

At the T-junction near Sewing Shields farm turn right and follow the track which soon curves left past Corner Cottage (see Notes, 1). Continue down into the valley and cross a cattle grid. After about half a kilometre you will cross another cattle grid and then the path curves to the right. Just before you reach a gate leading to Town Shields Farm, take the path that forks to the left, way-marked with a yellow arrow, and continue your walk in a northerly direction. At the ford, divert to take the foot-bridge on the left, and then return to the track. Go through the next gate and ascend the gentle hill. At the crest of the hill you get a view to the left of the picturesque Folly Lake (much photographed by those lucky enough to find it).

Walk on through the next gate to Halleypike Lough on your right.

Both these lakes provide a habitat for wildfowl including whooper swans and grebe, but you will need binoculars for any detailed identification. If you walk on a little further, you will get a good view of the Whin Sill outcrops beyond the lough (referred to in notes 2).

At this point you should turn round and start to re-trace your steps.

Immediately you will be able to see Corner Cottage on the horizon ahead. As you walk back you will have increasingly good views of Sewingshields Crags (see Notes, 2). Just after the foot-bridge, notice ahead the double arch of two lime kilns. As you get closer you will see that there is a path to allow you closer access (see Notes, 3).

> As you continue along the track on your return journey, you may notice on your OS map that there are historic fish ponds marked to the east of the path. There is no public access to this point on the marshy ground, but it is widely supposed that these ponds were put inside the foundation stones of Sewingshields Castle.

Retrace your footsteps to Sewing Shields farm (see Notes, 4) and thence back across the vallum to the old school and the permissive path to the Repeater Station.

Notes

1. At this point you are crossing the course of Hadrian's Wall (or the northern-most frontier of the Roman Empire). Nothing remains of the wall here as the stone was taken to build the farm house and outbuildings, as well as almost any other stone building in the vicinity. The farm was probably built on the site of Milecastle 35, of which there is now no sign. To the east of Corner Cottage is the site of a Wall turret.

2. Sewingshields Crags are an outcrop of the Whin Sill, which runs across the country from west to east, culminating at the Farne Islands. It is formed of a hard dark rock called dolerite and is an igneous intrusion in the limestone and sandstone. It was across this part of the Whin Sill that Hadrian chose to have his men build a wall. The sheer drop to the north side of this outcrop provided a natural barrier and obvious choice of location for a frontier wall (see Walk 20 for more information on the Whin Sill). Through a steep gap in the rocks, known as

Curlew

Shepherd's Pass, is the site of Sewingshields Castle. The date of erection is unknown but it belonged to John Heron of Chipchase in 1542 and was ruined then. There are many stories associated with this area, and Tomlinson's *Guide to Northumberland 1888*, which is still in print (Newgate Press 1999), cites at length the myths of the place. One such legend tells of King Arthur and his court, lying under the ruined castle waiting to be revived by any passing stranger blowing a bugle and picking up the waiting sword!

3. These are particularly good and complete lime kilns, with the little brick arches of the quick-lime 'eyes' still intact. Lime kilns are usually found close to where the limestone was quarried, and if you return to the main track and walk up behind the kilns you will see the quarry area. For more information on lime kilns see Walk 1.

4. The boulders around the foot of Sewing Shields Crags make an excellent hideaway and breeding ground for foxes. Many an exciting June evening can be spent with binoculars on the top of the crags, fox watching. Calm evenings in good visibility are best. Be prepared to be patient and make repeat journeys though, as the regular appearance of wildlife cannot be guaranteed. A good vantage point can be reached by walking west past the farm and the milecastle and onto the edge of the crags, keeping low to prevent your presence being detected from below. Take the **utmost care** however, as these crags are sheer. Do not wear anything noisy or smelly or bright, and, for safety, leave dogs and children at home!

Walk 12: Over Barcombe Fell

Route: Vindolanda east car park (Chesterholm), Crindledykes, Barcombe Fell, West End Town farm, Westwood, Chainley Burn, Vindolanda, Chesterholm.

Distance: 6km, 3¾ miles

High point: 264m

Ascent: 171m

Terrain: common, rough fields, lanes.

Refreshments: Twice Brewed Inn, about two miles west on Military Road, or Milecastle Inn, about four miles west on the Military Road.

Map: OS Explorer OL43

Take the Bardon Mill turn off the Military Road to the east of Vindolanda. Past the Crindledykes lime kiln the road bears right. Then take the next right to find the car park (marked Chesterholm on the OS map) at grid ref NY773665.

Walk out of the car park and turn left to go up the hill (see Notes, 1).

At the T-junction turn left and walk along to where the road forks.

> Here you can take a short diversion to Crindledykes communal lime kiln to your left (following the sign to Housesteads), which has an explanatory plaque naming this as one of the largest kilns of its type, having four quick-lime chambers. Short-Eared owls are known to nest in this kiln, so look out for them. The name Crindledykes means circular bank (from the remains of a Roman signalling station). For more information on lime kilns see Walk 1.

Return to the top road and turn right, then immediately left over a stile (see Notes, 2).

Follow the path as it zigzags up the Fell ahead. Where the path levels out, bear right, ignoring the path to the trig point. Then bear left towards a gap in the wall. From this point you are afforded good views to the south.

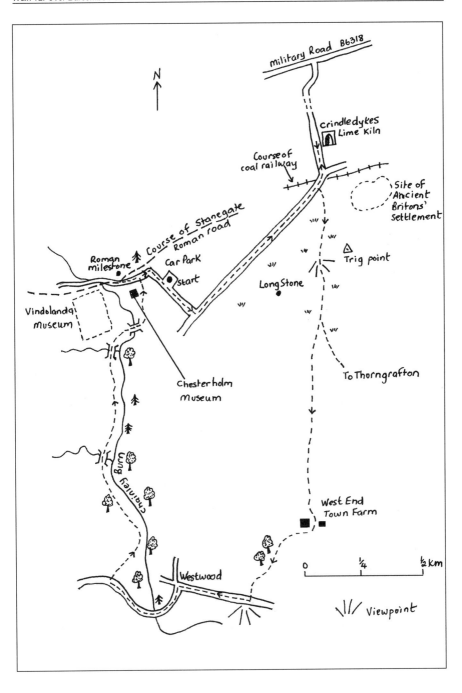

military Road B6318

N

Crindledykes
Lime Kiln

Course of
coal railway

Site of
Ancient
Britons'
settlement

Roman
milestone

Course of Stanegate
Roman road

Car Park

Start

Trig point

Long Stone

Vindolanda
Museum

Chesterholm
Museum

To Thorngrafton

Burn

Chainley Burn

West End
Town Farm

Westwood

0   ¼   ½ km

\|// Viewpoint

Ahead on the horizon you will see Catton Beacons (radio and television masts), and just to the left is Langley Smelt Mill chimney. In the foreground is Thorngrafton Common.

Follow the path down the south side of the Fell, aiming for the farmhouse in the bottom right hand corner of the Fell. At the wall, go through a gate and on down the track to another gate. Go through this and on until you reach the T-junction at West End Town Farm. Walk straight ahead through the gate of The White House and turn right. Go through the metal kissing gate. This area can be very boggy. Continue ahead and join the grassy track between a wall and the farmhouse. Where the wall on the left ends, turn left following the waymarker. Go down the bank with the line of trees on your right. Go over two stiles and bear right to aim for a gateway in the wall ahead. Go through this and keep to the right side of the field, following the path. Go over a wall stile, on the other side of which is a bench, where you may stop to rest and admire the view!

Turn right on the lane and pass through Westwood. At the cross-road turn left, and follow the road round until you reach a right turn to Vindolanda. Take this turn and ascend the lane. Where the road curves to the left, take the path to the right, way-marked to Vindolanda. This takes you through a gate and along a stony path towards riding stables. Keeping the buildings on your left, go through the gate and down into a dip with trees to your right.

Across the burn on your right, the Romans worked the hillside for lead.

Cross the footbridge adjacent to Fogrigg Ford and continue up the hill. Go through two more gates as you follow the path along the edge of the dene through which Chainley Burn flows. Go over a stile and then walk towards the boardwalk ahead.

Just before going onto the boardwalk, look up to the left to see a small section of re-constructed Roman Wall in Vindolanda Museum (see Notes, 3).

Continue along the route, crossing another footbridge, and go onto a narrow path which passes other parts of the museum, including a Roman temple and garden. The path leads you out along the museum exit, over a cattle grid and onto the lane. To return to your starting point, turn right here and walk back to the car park on the left. Alternatively you can take a short diversion by turning left after the cattle grid and walking down to the trees in the hollow, to see the course of the important Roman road, the Stanegate, where a Roman milestone still remains in situ, in the trees to the right of the lane.

Roman milestone on the Stanegate

Notes

1. Ahead is Barcombe Fell, on which lived a settlement of Ancient Britons. The position of the Chieftain's home, the pit dwellings of the followers and the cattle enclosures are still visible to the eastern side of the hill. Also on Barcombe are the quarries where the Romans obtained some of the stone for the Wall. Tracks used by the quarrymen to the Wall can still be followed. The Long Stone on the top of the hill marks the position where a quarryman lost his life in a quarry accident.

2. As well as stone quarries, Barcombe has been mined for coal over the years. Close to the stile you will see the course of a narrow gauge railway going under the road. This carried coal wagons down from Barcombe Pit into the valley.

3. Vindolanda was one of the original Roman forts, built about 300AD. There were two civilian settlements in the area at the time, and in the waterlogged conditions that prevail here, a remarkable series of finds of Roman antiquities have been superbly preserved. Vindolanda is an archaeological working site and has full-scale reconstructions of parts of the Wall, as well as housing Chesterholm and the museum – the largest Roman museum in the north, with its unique collection of Roman artefacts. However, the cache of Roman coins that was discovered by workmen in one of the Barcombe quarries in 1837, is now housed in Chesters Museum, a few miles east along the Military Road.

Walk 13: Portgate

Route: A68 at Plantation Cottage gate, Stagshaw Bank, Portgate, Fawcet Hill Cottage, Sandhoe, St Aidan's Chapel, A68.

Distance: 6km, 3¾ miles

High point: 245m

Ascent: 117m

Terrain: rough common, farmland, and lanes. 🐕

Refreshments: Errington Arms, north of the starting point on the A68. Vallum café, north-east of Corbridge on Military Road. St Oswald's Tea Room, north-west of Corbridge on Military Road

Map: OS Explorer OL43

This is a good walk to do in the winter months as the majority of the route is on country lanes. These have the advantage of being met-alled, making easy walking when the fields may be wet, and they are virtually traffic-free. They pass through tranquil countryside with sweeping views of Tynedale (see Notes, 1).

The walk starts at the lay-by on the north-bound side of the A68 north of Corbridge at grid ref NY987677. The official footpath starts at the entrance gate to Plantation Cottage, though there is a gate at the north end of the lay-by, which leads to the same path. From this gate take the path towards Portgate farm directly ahead. Where the path swings right towards a small wind turbine, branch off and continue to walk directly towards the farm. The path is not clear, but after you have passed under the power lines you will see a way-marked gate in the wall. Go through the gate and follow the path to cross Stagshawbank Burn. This section can be quite wet, but you can get through by stand-ing on the tussocks. Continue in the direction of the farm with the fence on your left, and pass through a gate gap. This route will take you round the right side of the farm complex to go over a stile on your left. Walk through the farm yard and continue straight ahead through the gate opposite, onto a metalled path (see Notes, 2)

Walk on for about 1km, passing through a gate on the way. At the

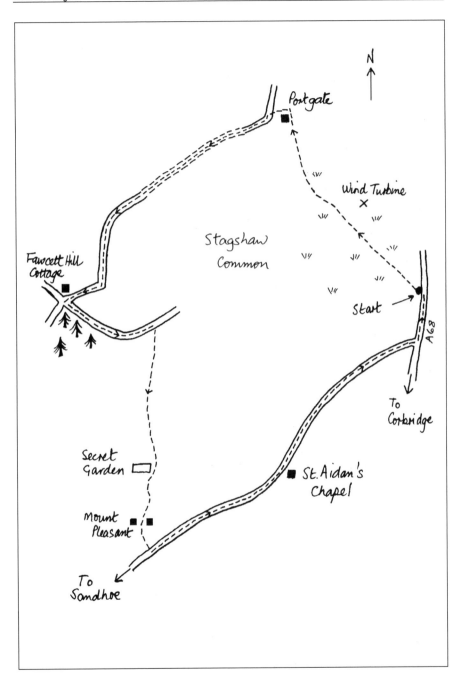

St Aidan's Chapel, Stagshaw

cross-road turn left towards Stagshaw High House. After about half a kilometre turn right into the field through a gate way-marked to Sandhoe. With the wall on your left, walk down the field to a gate which takes you into the next field. At the bottom of this field, go through a gate and you will see a secret garden on the right.

> The authors do not know the origin of this garden but there is a bench for the passing walker to sit and enjoy the view. The garden is sheltered and even in winter is a little oasis of colour and texture.

From here continue down the grassy path, and then go through the gate into the yard of Mount Pleasant. Follow the track between the buildings, and from here you can enjoy the view of a long meander of the River Tyne in the valley below, with Corbridge towards the left (see Notes, 3). At the road turn left and walk about half a kilometre until you reach St Aidan's Chapel on the right, which you could take time out to visit if you wish (see Notes, 4). From here continue along the road and turn left at the A68 to return to the starting point. Great care must be observed when walking along the A68 where traffic can be heavy and fast. Walk on the same side as the oncoming traffic.

Notes

1. Stagshaw to the north of Corbridge is documented as having an annual fair as early as 1293, and in its situation on the important Roman road Dere Street (the local section of Watling Street), has probably existed since Roman times. For centuries it has attracted visitors from as far afield as Scotland and Yorkshire. The main fair, for the sale of all types of domestic animal, was traditionally held on 4th July each year, but there were also other smaller fairs. According to Pevsner (Northumberland, Yale University Press 2001), two such 'wiste' fairs were held on 5th and 24th August, for the sale of lambs and ewes respectively. On 6th May, cattle and sheep were sold, and on Whitsun Eve, horses. Arising from the general chaotic, messy milieu of cattle, sheep, people and stalls etc. at Stagshaw Bank Fair, came an old-fashioned Newcastle saying: 'It's like Stagey Bank Fair', to describe a general mess!

2. The name Portgate probably means 'the steading on the market road'. Situated in the gap (old English, *geat*) where the Roman Wall crosses Dere Street.

3. Corbridge itself has probably existed since before Roman times, but held an important position for the Romans, so close to Hadrian's Wall and at the cross-roads of two ancient highways: the Stanegate and Watling Street. In subsequent centuries many of the buildings you can see today in Corbridge were built from Roman stone taken from Hadrian's Wall. This includes the Church, mentioned as early as 786, and which was probably founded by St Wilfrid. Parts of today's Church are Saxon, and the high arch in the tower is thought to have come from the nearby Roman fort and supply base, Corstopitum. The bridge at Corbridge was built in1674 and is the oldest bridge over the Tyne since the floods of 1771 swept away all others. Corbridge has two pele towers – an indication of its importance in the past.

4. St Aidan's Chapel was built in 1885 as a private chapel of the Straker family, who were, and still are well-known land-owners of the area. The architecture is of Decorated Gothic style, much favoured by the Victorians.

Walk 14: Corbridge Castles

Route: Corbridge, Milkwell Lane, Stagshaw Kennels, Halton Castle, Aydon Castle, Gallow Hill, Corbridge.

Distance: 9km, 6 miles

High point: 183m

Ascent: 161m

Terrain: farmland, wooded dene, and lanes. 🐕

Refreshments: there are several good pubs and cafes in the centre of Corbridge.

Map: OS Explorer OL43

This walk begins in Corbridge, outside the school on St Helen's Lane, grid ref NY993647. With your back to the school, walk left to the main road and turn left, walking for a short distance to take the first turn on the left. Almost immediately, take the left fork and walk along Milkwell Lane until you reach the two pottery bottle kilns on your right.

> The kilns are privately owned, but you are permitted to visit them by entering through the small garden gate (see Notes, 1).

Continue along the lane, and where the road fords the Cor Burn, cross by the footbridge. After about 1km you will pass Leazes Cottage on your right. At the T-junction turn right. At the way-marker to Low Houses, fork left, and ascend the stony lane. Where the lane curves left towards the houses, take a right fork through the trees and turn right onto the metalled lane. Just before the lane crosses Stagshawbank Burn, take the path on the right, way-marked to Halton, passing Stagshaw Kennels on your left.

> The foxhounds of the Tynedale Hunt are kennelled here, and there was mention of these kennels in Tomlinson's Guide of 1888.

Follow the path to cross the footbridge, bearing right and up the bank at the other side. Go through the way-marked gate on the left and walk up the bank keeping fairly close to the fence on the right. At the top, cross the stile and go right, walking along the edge of the field. Cross

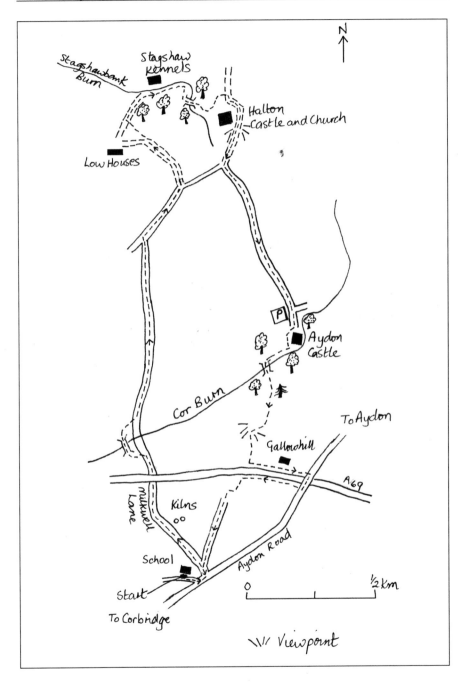

Bottle kiln

the ladder stile ahead, and at the cattle grid turn right on the metalled lane. Take the left fork keeping the ancient clipped yew hedge to your right. Soon you will have a panoramic view of the Tyne valley and beyond, as you pass Halton Castle, home of a county landowner, the church and ornamental duck-pond on the right (see Notes, 2).

Take time to visit the delightful Halton Church before taking the right fork past the graveyard and continue down the lane. At the T-junction bear left, following the sign to Aydon Castle.

After about 1km, where the lane turns left opposite Aydon Castle car park, walk straight on, to the castle on your left (see Notes, 3). Pass through two gates to skirt the walls of the castle and go down the ravine path to the footbridge across the Cor Burn. Climb up the other side, and, ignoring the padlocked gate at the top of the bank, follow the path through the trees, leaving the wood by a gate. Follow the path diagonally left across the field and through a way-marked gate. Turn left and walk close to the wall on your left, then through another gate onto a narrow path, which leads to the path above the A69. Turn left, and at the Aydon Road bridge turn right to cross the A69. Having crossed the dual-carriageway, turn right and go through the gate.

From here you can follow the narrow path alongside the A69 for a short distance and then all the way down to Corbridge. When you meet the Aydon Road turn right and then right again to return to the starting point.

Notes

1. These are the only bottle kilns to survive in the north-east and are now a scheduled monument. Walkers Pottery was a thriving industry here in the 18th/19th centuries, making pantiles and salt-glaze bricks. These typically purple bricks can still be seen in local buildings.

    Potteries usually arose where there was a local supply of clay, and that was the case here to the north of Corbridge. The local clay was used also by the nearby Jameson's Pipe Works, where drainpipes and troughs were made from 1910 until the 1970s.

2. Halton Castle is privately owned and comprises a 17th-century house built on to a 14th-century tower. The tower was built of Roman stone from Haltonchesters Fort, nearby to the north. Standing four storeys high, it is square with battlements and four round corner turrets, like those at Chipchase Castle, each turret containing a winding staircase. There are 13th-, 14th-, 15th- and 16th-century details in the buildings behind the tower, but the main house was added in 1696.

    The church, or Chapel of Ease, is constructed of Roman stones. A few Norman or even Saxon details remain in the structure of the church, but it was renovated and re-roofed in 1706. In the churchyard stands a Roman altar, which was moved from Aydon Road. Tradition has it that when a funeral passed the stone, the coffin had to be carried three times around the stone, hence its removal from a busy road!

    Halton takes its name from How Hyll – a lookout hill, where the Romans built a milecastle.

3. In architectural terms, Aydon Castle is very important as a fortified house rather than a castle. It is very rare in not having a keep. It is thought that the finishing touches were put to the building in 1305 when Robert de Reymes was granted a licence to crenellate it, but that the building actually predates that by two or three decades. Although protected on three sides by the deep ravine of the Cor Burn, it was captured in 1346 by David Bruce. In the 17th century it was functioning as a farm, but later reverted back to a domestic dwelling, which it remained until 1966. It is now run by English Heritage and is open to the public, and well worth a visit. The banks behind the castle are delightful with winter snowdrops and spring bluebells.

Walk 15: Hexham Sensory Garden

Route: Tyne Green, Chareway, Old Tannery, Sensory Garden, Gilesgate, Golf Club, River Tyne, Tyne Green.

Distance: 6.5km, 4¼ miles

High point: 66m

Ascent: 74m

Terrain: riverbank, streets, and woodland. 🐕

Refreshments: – there are several pubs and cafes in Hexham town centre.

Map: OS Explorer OL43

Start this walk at the car park at Tyne Green in Hexham, grid ref. NY936647 and walk west, away from Hexham Bridge. Pass the Tyne Green Golf Clubhouse and walk along the edge of the golf course, going over a footbridge, and continuing along the path close to the railway line on your left. Pass under the railway line at a tunnel on your left, and bear diagonally left across the green. Turn right at Chareway, with Ridley Terrace on the left of this road.

Soon you will see the old tannery on the left hand side of the road, straddling a burn, and opposite, on the right, is the old House of Correction (see Notes, 1).

Continue along the road past Foundry cottages and Foundry House on the right. Cross Eilansgate, and continue up the road ahead towards the pant (water fountain) dated 1858.

You are now in what was the tannery area of Hexham (see Notes, 2).

At Holy Island House take the right fork, and at the pub, The Old Tannery, turn right. Just before Ordley Terrace turn left over a bridge and walk up the hill. Where you join the path above, turn left towards the Abbey.

Hexham Abbey and its precincts are well worth a visit, and this would be a suitable point to leave the walk for a while to explore these buildings.

Returning to the walk, go through the gate on the left, just after the children's playpark, turn right, cross the ornamental bridge, and skirt the bowling green to approach Hexham House on the opposite side (see Notes, 3). To the left of Hexham House is the Sensory Garden. Take time to enjoy the peace here. (see Notes, 4).

With the Sensory Garden behind you, walk past Hexham House and bear left, going out through the gate in the wall to Gilesgate (originally Gilliegate).

Old Tannery straddling Cowgarth Burn

On the opposite side of the road is Hexham swimming pool, housed in a cleverly converted Victorian building that was originally another woollen warehouse.

Turn left and descend Gilesgate to cross Eilansgate, and re-trace your footsteps towards the railway. At the end of Chareway, cross the grass diagonally to the left and walk close to the wall with the railway on your right. At the far end of the grass, continue on the metalled path, and at the gate, take the footpath to the left, way-marked Spital Lane. Ascend the path, passing Hexham Golf Club building on your left and then a small gate to the practice green on the right. (see Notes, 5).

Continue to the way-marker to A69, where you turn right, and climb up through the trees, with views to your right of the Tyne valley and the village of Acomb. Skirt the golf course, keeping close to the fence on the right, then at a stile, descend through the wood to cross a foot-

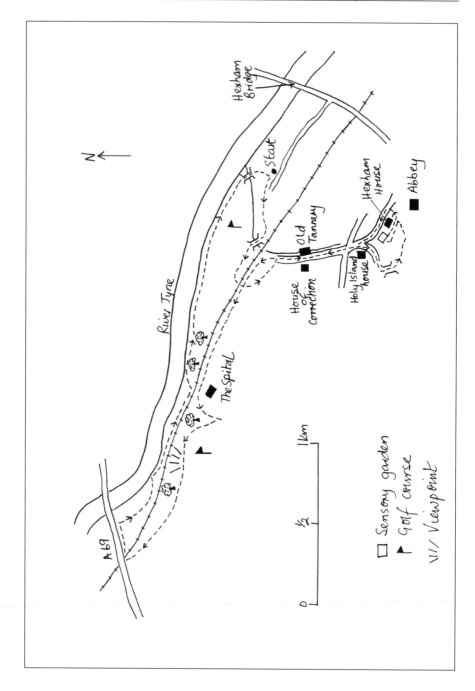

bridge. Go through the gate and up the steps to cross Constantine Bridge over the railway. Go down the steps at the other side, and just before the gate, turn left and curve back to the river (see Notes, 6). Walk to the right along the river bank for a short distance, and take the path on the right, which winds its way back through the trees towards the railway line path, where you turn left.

> This stretch of the river is a favourite haunt of the water birds merganser, goosander and goldeneye.

Just before the next gate, bear left and continue on the path with the railway on your right. Just before the start of Tyne Green Golf Course, go across to the left and walk along the river bank path with the golf course on your right. After about 1km, just after the children's playpark, cross over the grass on your right, to return to the car park.

Notes

1. The building spanning the Cowgarth Burn is an early 19th-century tannery, and latterly Henry Bell's Woollen warehouse. Presumably its position so close to the water gave access for washing the skins. The House of Correction opposite, with its slit windows, gives us an idea of how prisoners were treated in the early 19th century. The cells are on the first floor and still have their wall shackles and heavy iron doors.

2. This is the oldest, and used to be the poorest, part of Hexham and was for some time in history known as 'the Misery'. It was the centre of the tanning industry between the 16th and 18th centuries, with many of the street and building names reflecting this – Tanners Row, Skinners Arms, Glovers Place. Hexham was famous for fine glove-making during this time, and some of the history is told in the café, the Hexham Tans, in St Mary's Chare. Holy Island House (1667) is a lovely example of Elizabethan architecture, with other notable houses of slightly later dates around it. The pant is Victorian and ornamental, but it reflects the tradition of Northumbrian watering places, usually made of sandstone, with a trough for animals, situated at a place where a natural spring rises. If the water is constantly flowing, it is known as a running pant. This one is, unfortunately, dry.

3. Hexham House was built originally as the town house of Lord Allendale. In 1904 the then Lord, gifted the accompanying land known as the Sele, to the people of Hexham for their recreation. The building is now used as

council offices. The covering of wisteria blossom on the south wall is superb in the spring, and quite exceptional so far north.

4. The Sensory Garden is owned by Hexham council and was restored in 2004/5 by a local group under the guidance of the course leader, Jonathon Archer, for Newcastle College (Hexham campus). It is designed to appeal to all the senses, not just the visual.

5. Hexham Golf Club is housed in a rather splendid building, the Spital, only the name of which, gives a hint of its original purpose. It was built in about 1802, on the site of the medieval St Giles' leper Hospital. Before becoming the present golf clubhouse, it was in the hands of Sir Loftus Bates and the Robb family.

6. On the opposite bank of the river is a modern-looking house, greatly altered from its original structure. In the 19th century this was all railway land, and the house opposite comprised railway cottages. A glance down-river will also reveal another relic from the Victorian railway era. You will see the remains of a railway bridge which carried the Border Counties Railway line running from Hexham to Riccarton Junction, by Keilder.

Walk 16: Warden Hill Fort

Route: Bridge End, Quality Cottages, Laverick Plantation, Fort on Warden Hill, High Warden, Warden, Bridge End.

Distance: 6km, 3¾ miles

High point: 174m

Ascent: 158m

Terrain: farmland, woodland, and lane. 🐕

Refreshments: The Boatside, Warden

Map: OS Explorer OL43

Park somewhere near the Boatside pub just north of the A69, on the west side of Hexham, at grid ref. NY909660. Walk north along the road signed to Chesters and Chollerford. Very soon, the road passes under a railway bridge and then there is a lay-by on the left. At the way-marker in the lay-by, turn left along the path and walk alongside the railway line until you reach Quality Cottages. Take the path to the right, way-marked to Fourstones. Go through a gate and continue ahead, keeping the fence to your left.

> Before going through the next gate it is worth turning round to admire the view of Tynedale from this vantage point in the fork between the North Tyne and the South Tyne Rivers.

Go through the gate and turn left. When you reach the field, continue upwards, skirting to the right of the woodland. Go through two more gates, keeping close to the fence on your left. Go through the next gate and walk along with the woods on your right, and then follow the path into and through the woods. Just before the gate at the end of this section of woodland, turn back on yourself to the right, following the way-marker to Warden. Go through the next gate, which brings you out into the open, with Warden Hill before you (see Notes, 1). Walk to your left around the hill, gradually climbing towards the summit. Work your way to the south-east side of the hill, where a gate in the wall will take you through to a trig point. With your back to the trig point, walk down the field ahead, keeping close to the wall on your

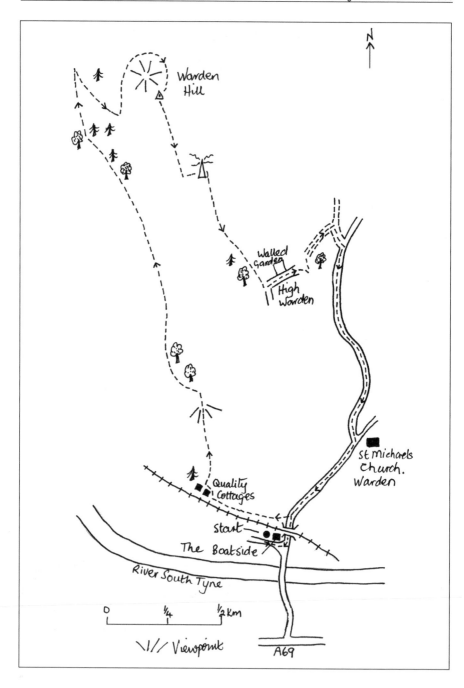

N

Warden
Hill

Walled
Garden

High
Worden

St michaels
Church.
Warden

Quality
Cottages

Start

The Boatside

River South Tyne

0   ¼   ½ km

\|// Viewpoint

A69

left. At the end of the wall go through the gate on your left following the way-marker, and walk along until you come to the gate on your right which will lead you through to the telephone mast. Pass the mast and continue on the main track down the hill. This track leads you to a gate onto a double-walled path with woodland on your right. Turn left at the Warden way-marker, and walk past a walled garden on your left in High Warden.

Most of this hamlet is the property of a local landowner.

After passing between buildings to the next way-marker, go left towards Warden and then immediately take the right fork. At the cattle grid, go through the gate and continue down the metalled drive. Turn right at the next way-marker and then right again after the cattle grid onto the road, and walk back down the lane to Warden. Just before returning to your starting point, it is worth visiting the church of St Michael and All Angels on the left (see Notes, 2).

Notes

1. The name Warden means Watch Hill, and you can certainly see why ancient communities would have chosen this point for a fort, with panoramic views allowing plenty of fore-warning in case of attack. The ridges you see around the summit of the hill are the remains of an Iron-Age Hill Fort. There is evidence of other hill forts in the area on the hill tops above Wall village to the north. From this vantage point you have 360° views. Look for Chesters Roman fort and Chollerford Bridge in the middle distance to the north-west.

2. The tower of St Michael's Church is Saxon with the belfry probably added in the 1760s along with the sundial. As with many ancient buildings in this part of Northumberland, some of the stone is known to be Roman, brought from Hadrian's Wall and its associated fortresses. The transepts are 13th century

Lych-gate at St Michael's Church

with 19th-century arches and the present chancel dates from 1889 as does much of the stained glass. The ornately carved wooden lych-gate was added in 1903. In the churchyard is a rough stone cross thought to be the Warden Village Cross from the 7th century.

Walk 17: Haughton Castle

Route: Humshaugh, Lincoln Hill, Heatheridge, Keepershield, Coldwell, Wester Hall, Haughton Castle, Humshaugh.

Distance: 9km, 5½ miles

High point: 146m

Ascent: 108m

Terrain: fields, lanes. 🐕

Refreshments: The Crown Hotel, Humshaugh, Riverside Café by garage at Chollerford Bridge, George Hotel Chollerford.

Map: OS Explorer OL43

The walk starts in the centre of Humshaugh village north of Hadrian's Wall about seven miles from Hexham. There is room to park in the centre of the village near the Crown Pub at grid ref. NY920715. With your back to the pub, turn right and walk west along the road. There are some very old houses along this road worthy of note (see Notes, 1).

At the cross-road, walk ahead onto a grassy path, which soon joins a metalled lane where you bear right and walk past Halfway Houses to the hamlet of Lincoln Hill. Some metres on, after the mast on your left, where the road curves to the left, turn right to go through a way-marked gate. Cross a small stream and follow the path as it gently ascends to a gate. Go through the gate and walk along the left edge of the field, continuing to the next gate and next field. At the end of this field turn left through a gate and walk along the right-hand side of the field. Go through two gates and pass a spring on the right. Continue ahead, keeping to the right-hand side of the field. Go through the next gate and field, at the end of which, you should turn right onto a metalled lane, passing West Heatheridge Cottage. The next building you reach is Heatheridge House. Here, follow the lane round to the left, and at the road turn left.

Take care walking along this road and notice the pant (water fountain) on the left, similar in style to the one in Humshaugh.

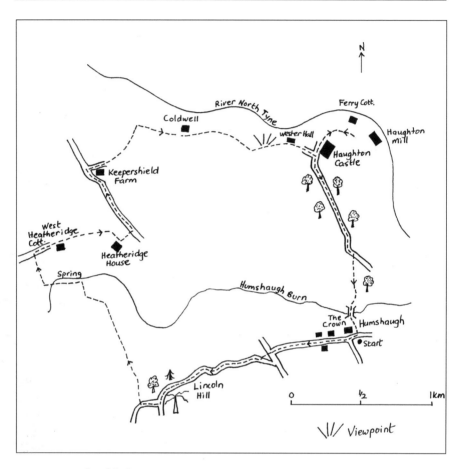

At Keepershield farm turn immediately right, following the sign to Haughton. Pass Coldwell farm on the left (see Notes, 2). Continue along the lane and soon the River North Tyne will come into view in the valley to your left with the village of Barrasford in the middle distance.

> Soon you will pass Wester Hall on your left, a former vicarage with an interesting early 18th-century summer house in the garden.

At the T-junction turn left to have a better look at Haughton Castle (see Notes, 3).

> Opposite the castle, on the other side of the wall is the remains of a

Haughton Castle

walled garden which must have been splendid in its day. The chimney in the wall at the far side is still visible as an indication of the heating system in the hollow walls, against which glass houses would have been built to grow exotics such as peaches, grapes and figs.

If you cross the cattle grid and walk down the road for a little way you will be able to get better views of the castle and also of the Ferry Cottage to the left, by the river, and then Haughton Mill a little further along the river bank (see Notes, 4).

Retrace your steps to the Wester Hall junction and bear left along the lane heading south. Go through a metal kissing gate on the right, when you reach the way-marker to Humshaugh. Walk diagonally across the field and go through the gate opposite. Walk along the field keeping the fence to your right and then go through the kissing gate into the wood. Follow the path to cross a foot-bridge and gate. Walk straight ahead across the final field and through the gate, which leads you between houses onto the lane where you started the walk.

Notes

1. Dale house on your right, dated 1664, is thought to be the oldest house in the village. It has stone mullioned windows, as does Teesdale House (1690). Dale House is a reconstructed bastle house, altered in the 17th century when the need for fortified homes in the borders subsided. Linden House on the other side of the road was originally two bastle houses from the 16th century. For more information on bastle houses see Walk 9. The Evans Alms house, bearing the inscription 'St David's Day1864', has a pant (water fountain) built into its garden wall. This Victorian structure is of a similar style to one you will see on the roadside later in the walk.

2. The Coldwell farm buildings look like they have not changed much over the years. Because of this they are a favourite location for the filming of Catherine Cookson stories. The farm is also well-known for the breeding of Clydesdale horses, and if you are lucky you may be able to see some of these beautiful animals in the field opposite (for more information on Clydesdale working horses see Walk 4).

3. Haughton Castle dates from the 13th century but it has been greatly altered and added to over the centuries. It is an extremely imposing building, having been restored from ruin by the owner, William Smith, in about 1770. At that time it was restored in keeping with its original ancient structure, though the interior was greatly modified in Victorian times under the instruction of the well-known local architect John Dobson. The walls are eight feet thick and the castle holds an imposing position high above a great meander in the river. Legend maintains that it was at Haughton Castle where Archie, head of the Border Reiver Armstrong clan, starved to death having been thrown into the dungeon and forgotten by Sir Thomas Swinburne.

4. Ferry Cottage marks the place where until very recent times a primitive rope and pulley system transported a ferry across the river. This is known to have been in use continually since the reign of Henry II (before 1189). The last woman to work the ferry, before its closure in the 1960s, still lives in the cottage today. Haughton Mill, a little further along the river bank, was a paper mill built in 1788 by the then owner of the castle. It was here that, under the instruction of the Prime Minister William Pitt, forged French 'assignats' (paper currency) were manufactured during the Napoleonic wars, to be infiltrated into the French economy in order to lower the value of the currency.

Walk 18: Simonburn

Route: Simonburn, Castle Lane, Castle Dene, Fenwickfield, Castle Burn, Pit Wood, Ward Lane, Red Burn, Simonburn.

Distance: 8km, 5 miles

High point: 224m

Ascent: 164m

Terrain: Woods, fields, lanes. A few difficult stiles ut there are farm gates close by, which you must shut. 🐕

Refreshments: Black Bull and Battlesteads Inn, Wark, The Crown Hotel, Humshaugh; tea shop, Simonburn.

Map: OS Explorer OL43

The walk starts in Simonburn village, three miles south of Wark, just off the B6320. Park in the car park to the left of the Church at grid ref. NY871736. Walk past the gate at the front of the Church and continue along the village green to the cross-road, where you turn left along Castle Lane. Where the road curves to the right, turn left over a little bridge and then left again, following the way-marker to Fenwickfield. Ascend the track through the woods. Where the path levels out a little you will see the remains of Simonburn Castle on your right (see Notes, 1).

Continue on the stony track and go through a gate. The ascent becomes gentler now for about one kilometre, until you reach the next gate and then Fenwickfield farm. Walk to the left of the farm and continue to the gate ahead by the trees. Go through the gate and bear diagonally right towards the corner of a fence. Follow the yellow arrow in a westerly direction towards a lone tree ahead. Soon you will see a marker post to the left of the tree, so aim for this.

When you reach the marker, turn right and walk along the bridleway. Cross a drainage channel and go through a gate ahead. Continue up to the brow of the hill and then descend to a ford, which you can cross at stepping stones. Bear towards the left of the trees of Pit Wood ahead.

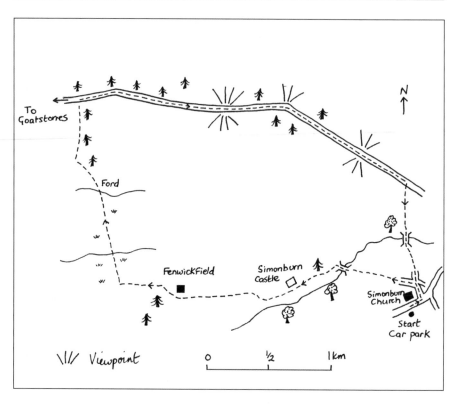

To Goatstones

Ford

Fenwickfield

Simonburn Castle

Simonburn Church

Start Car park

N

\|// Viewpoint

0   ½   1km

Go through a gate in the corner of the field and turn right onto the metalled farm lane, walking up to a gate and then the lane.

Our walk continues to the right, but if you would like to visit the four-poster stone circle of Goatstones you should turn left here and walk along the lane, passing the entrance to Goatstones farm, and continue to a public footpath on the left which leads you to the stones beyond Ravensheugh Crags. The return trip will add about 4km to your walk. Alternatively you could return by car at the end of your walk. There are four stones forming a circle, one of very few to be found south of Perthshire. The name is thought to originate from 'Gyet Stones' meaning wayside stones, as they are close to an old drovers' track.

If you are not walking to Goatstones, turn right onto the lane. After a short ascent, you will begin a gradual pleasant descent along the lane, which affords you beautiful views to north and south in the breaks between plantations. To the north you will see North Tynedale and the river which names it. The castle which you will see to the north after about one and a half kilometres is Chipchase Castle (see Notes, 2).

After another kilometre turn right over a stile, following the way-marker to Simonburn.

> This stile is difficult for dogs, but there is a farm gate nearby which you must be sure to shut.

Walk down the field with the hedge on your right. Cross the foot-bridge and then a stile and walk ahead

Simonburn village

across the next field. When you reach a fence, continue with it on your right. At the end of the field, cross the gated foot-bridge, and continue straight on ascending the field. At the top, keep the fence to your left and continue in the same direction. In the corner of the field, go through a gate and continue with the hedge on your right. Go through the final gate and walk between the buildings to emerge by the tea shop on the village green. Walk on past the Church (see Notes, 3) to return to the start.

Notes

1. The castle probably dates from 1186, for Simon of Senlis, Earl of Northumberland, who had to defend North Tynedale (260 square miles, stretching from Carter Bar to the Roman Wall) against his stepfather, King David of Scotland. In 1541 it housed a garrison of one hundred men for the Keeper of Tynedale. It belonged to the Herons of Chipchase and

then the Allgoods of Nunwick who partially restored it in 1766. Today only part of the north-east tower remains with walls over nine feet thick, and the ruin has been listed as being in need of urgent attention. Legend has it that treasure was buried within the walls and the good folk of the parish were mainly responsible for its present condition in their fruitless frenzy to find riches.

2. Chipchase Castle was formerly a hunting ground of the Umfravilles, Lords of Prudhoe, after the Norman conquest. In the 14th century it belonged to the Herons. Even from this distance you can see the 14th-century Pele tower to the left and the additional Jacobean Mansion, built in 1621 to the right. The mansion is said to be one of the best examples of its type in the country. The grounds and castle are open occasionally throughout the summer.

3. It is thought that St Mungo brought Christianity in C6. He was Bishop of Strathclyde in a village called Glesgu (now Glasgow). He died in 601. The present church predates 1208. The floor to the east side of the nave falls to the east, following the natural slope of the ground. Even in the 13th century this was very rare. The pillars increase slightly in height from west to east to allow for this. Since the choir was altered in 1229 and there was a papal interdict preventing any new church being built from 1208-13, it is more than likely that the pillars have been supporting the nave roof from well before 1215 when King John signed Magna Carta. Moreover the choir axis inclines to the north – a 13th-century aid to show how Christ's head fell to one side on the cross.

The earliest remains of a Christian settlement are to be found in the porch. These are remnants of an Anglian cross of the Tyne Valley school, begun by Italian workmen brought to Hexham by St Wilfrid in 690. This cross is of either 8th or 9th century. Simonburn churchyard is the resting place of the ancestors of the local land-owning family, the Allgoods, who own almost all of Simonburn village. The Rectory, next to the Church, was in use in 1541. It was rebuilt by the Reverend Major Allgood in 1666, and the Georgian façade was added in 1725. Interesting features of the Rectory include: the coal furnaces built into the north wall of the kitchen garden; the window where the Reverend Wastell's wife carved her name with her diamond ring 250 years ago; the three-seated 18th-century lavatory and the twelve lime trees planted by the Reverend Wastell in celebration of the defeat of the Jacobites (lime being the badge of the House of Orange). Apart from one that fell in 1972, all the trees remain and are known locally as the twelve apostles.

Walk 19: Goodwife Hot (Wark)

Route: Wark village green, Wark Bridge, Blindburn, High Carry House, Birtley Shields, Piper Lane, Birtley, Warkshaugh Bank, Old Wark Station, Wark Bridge, Wark village green.

Distance: 8km, 5 miles

High point: 212m

Ascent: 145m

Terrain: farmland, lanes.

Refreshments: Black Bull and Battlesteads Inn, Wark.

Map: OS Explorer OL43

Begin the walk at Wark village green, grid ref NY 861771where there is plenty of room for parking. Walk in an easterly direction out of the village over the bridge across the North Tyne.

Wildfowl are frequently found along this stretch of the river, including Canada geese.

Turn left, following the sign to Birtley, bear right by the first cottage and ascend the hill. As the road curves to the right near the top of the hill, take the left turn signed to Low Carry House and walk along the lane, crossing a cattle grid. Just after crossing the small stream of Blind Burn, as you approach a gate, ignore the left fork off the road and go through the gate. Continue along the lane until you have passed Thorneyhirst on your left.

The grassy patch on the left is a good place to stop for a viewpoint (see Notes, 1).

At the T-junction turn right, way-marked to High Carry House and continue to a gate and a stile. Go through the gate to the left and continue the ascent along the track. Pass through Birtley Shields farmyard and two gates and continue along the farm road. At the fork, go left, ignoring the two signs to Birtley. At the T-junction turn right into Birtley.

Notice the Manor House on your right with its beautiful stone mullioned windows. There is an ancient plaque built into the wall of the house with

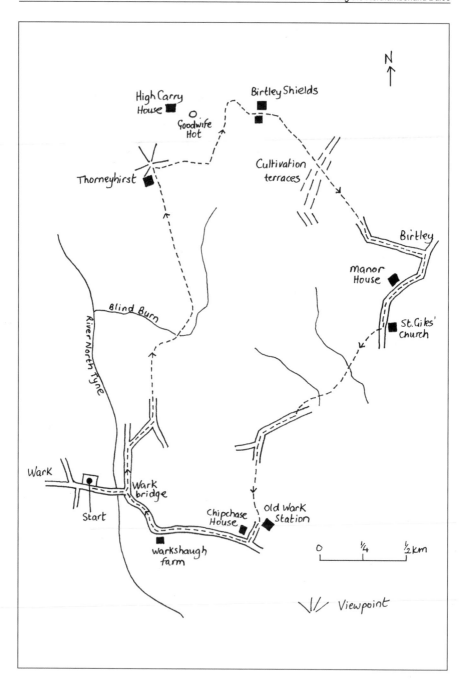

Manor House at Birtley

the name of Thomas Robson carved on it. This name appears several times in the churchyard further on and was obviously a local family name for several generations.

Continue along the road to the Church of St Giles on the left (see Notes, 2). On leaving the church, cross the road and follow the narrow way-marked path ahead. Cross a stile and walk across the field, going slightly to the left towards a gap in the trees. Follow the descending grassy path bearing towards the left and go over a stile and a ditch. Then ascend the other side. Stay with the path as it goes down again, keeping the fence on your left. Aim for the gate ahead on your left, picking a path through to avoid the more marshy places. Go through the gate and turn right onto the road. Where the road curves to the right, fork left on the lane ahead. As you descend Warkshaugh Bank, look out for the railway buildings and station platform as you approach the disused Hexham/Rickerton Junction railway line, which was closed in the 1950s. Follow the lane round, keeping the old station house on your left and walk down to the bottom of the hill. At the T-junction turn right past Chipchase House which was formerly an inn. Continue along the road, passing Warks Haugh Farm (see Notes, 3).

As you approach the village, notice the modern and commendable innovation of solar-powered street lights.

Turn left to cross the bridge and re-trace your footsteps to the village green, passing the grand Victorian Town Hall (formerly the Mechanics Institute) on the left.

Notes

1. Looking across the valley on your left you will see a white house called Houxty. This was formerly the home of the Northumbrian naturalist Abel Chapman who wrote books on the North Tyne area. To your right is High Carry House with its ruined pele tower. This whole area is littered with earthworks and many Iron Age Hill Forts. Further right, on top of the hill is Birtley Shields Farm, and beyond it are Iron Age cultivation terraces. Just to the right of High Carry House is a small pointed hill, known locally as Goodwife Hot. There are many theories as to the origin of this name, including that she was the goddess of fertility. Local historian Godfrey Watson devotes the title of his well-recommended book of Northumbrian place names to this Goodwife, whoever she was.

2. St Giles' Church has several features of architectural interest. The oldest parts of the church are Norman (notice the round arches), but other parts, such as the stained glass windows, are Victorian. If you stand outside, facing the front of the church you will notice that the graveyard to the left (north) side of the church is higher than that to the right (south). It was traditional to bury the common people on the dark, northern side of some churches, whereas the gentry were buried on the sunny south side. Obviously there were far more commoners than gentry, so the graveyard to the north became much fuller. This church illustrates the point very well! The grave covers in the entrance porch are medieval and the carving is quite clearly defined. The sword for a man, and scissors for a woman are easily recognisable.

3. There are several old bastle houses in this area, and Warks Haugh farm is a good example. Notice the door at first floor level, which would formerly have been accessible by retractable ladder only. When life on the borders calmed down and there was no longer danger of attack from the Border Reivers, the inhabitants of this old bastle built stone steps up to the entrance door. For more information on bastles see Walk 9.

Walk 20: Thockrington

Route: Fell House, Carrier's Lane, Little Swinburne, Short Knowes, Thockrington, Carrier's Lane, Fell House.

Distance: 7.5km, 4¾ miles

High point: 222m

Ascent: 93m

Terrain: farmland, lanes. 🐕

Map: OS Explorer OL43

Start this walk on the B6342, to the north-west of Hallington reservoir, near Fell House at grid ref. NY 960769. The grass verge is wide enough to park just north of Fell House, but take care as it can be a busy road. Walk south-east towards Fell House on your left, and turn right opposite Fell House to go through a gate way-marked to Thockrington. Walk diagonally to the right across the field and go through the gate in the opposite corner. Continue straight on, keeping close to the fence on the left. At the next gate, go through onto Carrier's Lane and turn left. Follow this track to Little Swinburne farm (see Notes, 1). Enter the farm yard through two gates and follow the track as it curves to the right just before a row of cottages.

> As you look towards the tallest farm building from here, behind it is an outcrop of the Whin Sill which runs the width of the country, and upon certain ridges of which, Hadrian's Wall was built. Whin stone is actually quartz dolerite, a hard, dark stone, and as you continue on this walk you will see further outcrops of the Whin Sill. For more information on the Whin Sill, see Walk 11.

Continuing along the track, you will pass the now ruined buildings of Swinburne Pele on the right and then Short Knowes on your left. Go through the next gate and, at the sign to Thockrington, turn right, continuing on through two more gates towards Thockrington Church. Enter St Aidan's Church by going through the farm gate on your left in front of the church, and then through the little churchyard gate (see Notes, 2).

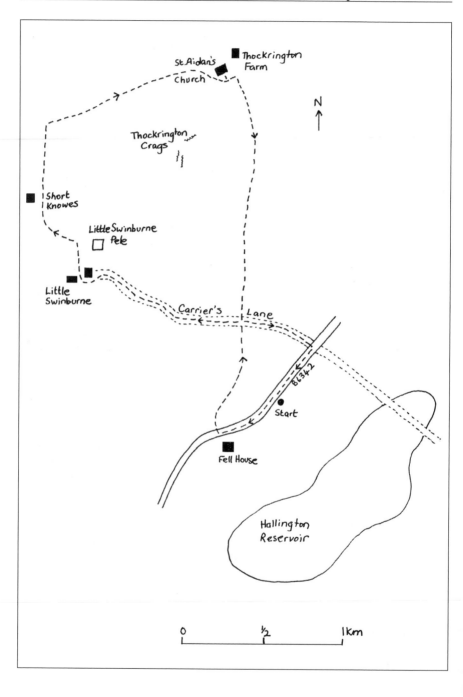

St Aidan's Church, Thockrington

Lord Beveridge (the architect of the National Health Service) is buried in this churchyard, his daughter being married into the Burns family at nearby Carrycoats Hall.

Leave the churchyard by the little gate and turn left, walking close to the wall, and exit by the gate ahead. Turn left onto the lane and, almost immediately, go through the gate on the right. Take the bridleway to the left, way-marked to Colwell, making your way across the field keeping the wall to your left.

To your left you will have a view of Bavington Folly (shown as a dovecote on the OS map), but built intentionally as a folly by the local landowners of Bavington Hall.

Follow the wall in a southerly direction through two gates to the Carrier's Lane. Turn left and follow the grassy track over the field to the road. Turn right and walk carefully along the road, facing the oncoming traffic, to return to your car parking position.

In winter months the surrounding fields are a favourite haunt of flocks of lapwings and mistle thrushes.

Lapwing

Notes

1. On the right are the ruins of Little Swinburne Pele. The tallest of the farm buildings is probably a reconstructed pele tower, and the building in front of it resembles a bastle. See notes on peles and bastles in Walk 2 – Mohope and Walk 9 – Old Haydon. Note the large corner stones, and small, high windows, typically built for defence during the time of the Border Reivers.

2. The story goes that in days gone by, a serviceman returning to his native village of Thockrington brought the plague to the village and subsequently every member of the settlement died. All the buildings, except the church, were knocked down, and their remains can be seen, grassed over, by looking over the back wall of the churchyard.

3. St Aidan's Church is Norman in origin with several additions and alterations in subsequent centuries. It is thought to have been built by the Umfraville family. The first Umfraville, a Norman baron, was granted large swathes of land in Northumberland by William the Conqueror.

4. A little way to the north of the Church is Houky Hill, one of very few sites in Northern England where the white-flowered umbelliferous plant, spignel can be located. Lunn (2004) tells us of its powerfully aromatic scent, and Halliday (1997) reveals that it is sought after in London as an aphrodisiac!

Walk 21: Nooks and Crannies of Hexhamshire

Route: Dipton Mill, Dotland Park, Black Hall, Whitley Mill, Mollersteads, Juniper, Lee, Newbiggin, Letah Woods, Dipton Mill.

Distance: 11km, 7 miles (or 8km, 5 miles)

High point: 182m

Ascent: 175m

Terrain: fields, woodland, lanes. 🐕

Refreshments: Dipton Mill Inn

Map: OS Explorer OL43

This 7-mile walk comprises two circular walks put together. If you would prefer a shorter walk of about 5 miles, you can omit the Black Hall/Mollersteads/Dye House loop by taking the stile on your left after the vantage point on page 95, marked ▸ and resuming the instructions at the point marked with ▸▸ on page 96.

Start the walk at the Dipton Mill pub, about 2 miles south of Hexham at grid ref NY 929610. There is room to park opposite the pub. With your back to the pub entrance, cross the road and walk straight ahead along the track. Cross a lane and continue ahead into Dotland Park Farm.

> As you approach Dotland Park, notice the woodland banks on your right. These are covered in swathes of snowdrops in January and February. The ancient house is also noteworthy (see Notes, 1). Look at the old windows in the gable end of the house by the barn.

Follow the path to the right, passing in front of the barn and then continue along the main farm track away from the farm, passing through a series of gates until you reach a field. Walk diagonally to the right across the field until you reach a small, ditch-like burn, and then continue along with the burn on your right as far as the fence. Cross the footbridge on the right and walk to the stile. Go over the stile and turn left onto the lane. Walk for about 200m until you have passed

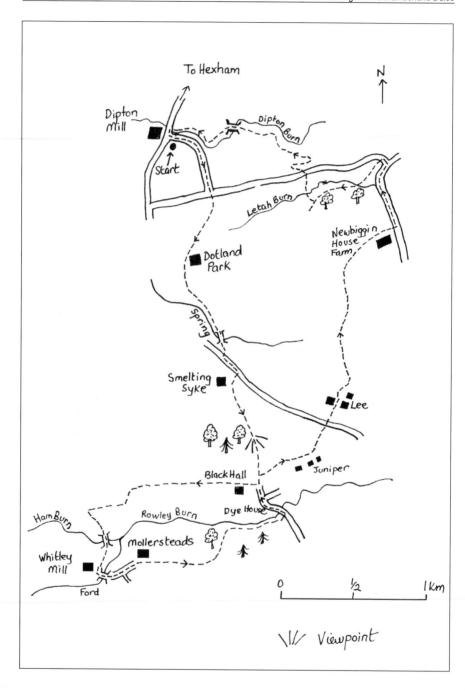

Smelting Sike buildings on your right. Immediately after the entrance, go through the gate on the right, by the way-marker to Juniper. Cross the field to a gate opposite. Go through the gate and, bearing left, walk along the side of the field with the wall on your left. Go through a gate and continue along the side of the next field. At the end of this field, go through a kissing gate and continue along the narrow path edging the trees of Blackhall Wood on your right. Go through a gate and walk along the field, keeping close to the wall on your left.

▸ It is worth stopping to take in the views from this vantage point (see Notes, 2).

For the shorter walk, where the wall ends at a stile on your left, stop, and resume the instructions at ▸▸ on page 96.

For the longer walk: where the wall ends, bear slightly right towards a stile to the right of an ancient hawthorn and holly hedge. Go over the stile and walk along the short path that leads you to stone steps down a wall onto a lane. Turn right and walk past Black Hall Farm house on your left. Go through the gate in front of you and on to the track. After going through the next gate, walk slightly to the right of the rise in the field ahead and then head towards the next gate in a wall. After passing through this gate, walk straight ahead across the middle of a long field. Ahead you will find some way-marked steps built into the wall. Cross these into a spinney, and cross the next wall into a field.

From here bear diagonally left towards a marker post and cross the stream by stepping stones. Follow the path ahead, which curves to the right after a short distance, towards the next marker post. Continue along the path. Soon the path drops down, to the left. Walk down this hollow towards a foot-bridge, and cross over the Rowley Burn. Turn left, go through the next gate and bear right towards the next stile. Cross the stile and then take the left path, which follows along the side of Devil's Water. Go over the next stile and under a foot-bridge, passing Whitley Mill on your right. Cross the water at the next foot-bridge and bear left at the lane. Where the lane curves to the right, walk straight ahead, following a sign to Mollersteads (see Notes, 3). Just before the farm, go through a gate on the right, and take the left path, way-marked to Steel Farm. Go through a gate and along the field ahead, passing Mollersteads, to the next gate. Go through this gate and walk part-way along the next field until you reach a stile on the right. Cross the stile and turn left, continuing along the side of the field with the hedge on your left. When you reach a stile ahead, cross it and cross the ditch, turning left into the woods.

Follow the woodland track downhill. Bear right with the path. After a short distance cut through the trees to your left until you reach the path at the water's edge. Bear right and follow the path along the Devil's Water until you reach a road. Turn left and cross the bridge, following the road as it curves to the right through the hamlet of Dye House. As the road bends right again, take the narrow way-marked footpath ahead, and ascend to a gate. Go through the gate and cross the field ahead, towards a gate in the wall. Go through the gate, cross the Black Hall Farm lane and climb the stone steps in the wall that you came down earlier in the walk. Continue ahead and go over the stile, bearing right past the hawthorn and holly hedge towards a stile at the corner of the wall.

▸▸ **For the short walk, skip to here; both walks continue from this point:** Go over this stile and through the gate into a field. Walk along the edge of the field with the fence to your right. Then branch left towards a stile at the left of the building ahead. Go over this and two more stiles as you follow the path above the hamlet of Juniper, which eventually comes to the end of a field. Ignore the gate ahead and turn left and walk towards the cottage. Go through the way-marked gate at the cottage and turn right and then immediately left after the cottage to go through another gate. Follow the path along the left side of the field, although you may have to divert to the right for a little way to avoid a boggy patch, and then go through the gate on the left.

Cross the lane and walk straight ahead following a way-marker to Newbiggin. Soon you will reach the hamlet of The Lee. In this tiny hamlet, turn left onto a grassy track immediately before a house called Barnleenook. Go through the makeshift gate on the left into a field and turn right, walking round the edge of the field with the fence to your right. Go through the next gate and then two more fields and two more gates, with the fence on your right all the way. At the next 'd, continue in the same direction following the path, until you 'ain to a fence on your right. Continue on and through a gate, and follow the line of beech trees on your right. Go over a stile, and walk diagonally to the right across the field towards Newbiggin House Farm. Go through the gate onto the metalled track, and through the farm yard and turn left at the road. Walk along the road until it curves to the right, after which you turn left over a bridge (see Notes, 4) and then first left again through a gate into Letah Wood.

Follow the path through the wood. The path soon diverts left to the Letah Burn which you cross. Be aware that these woodland paths can be very slippery after rain.

> In the spring, these woods are richly carpeted in wild daffodils. This is thought to be one of the most northerly habitats for wild daffodils.

Keeping the burn on your right, follow the path to the highest point. Before losing any height, pick up a narrow track on your right and walk down the steep slope and cross the Letah Burn again. Climb up the other side, bear left, and when you reach a wider track turn right and continue your ascent. At the lane turn right and then immediately left over a stile way-marked to Dipton Mill and Hexham.

From here, look down the slope to a gate diagonally to your left. This is where you should aim for, but you will need to make a zigzag path downwards, going first left then right. When you reach the gate go over the adjacent stile and continue along the path with Dipton Burn to your right.

> This is often a good spot to sight a heron.

At the end of the field cross the footbridge, ignore the stile ahead of you, and take the path to the left, with the burn now to your left.

> The path you are now walking along is lined with blackthorn bushes, which give a glorious display of white blossom in the spring and sloes in the autumn.

Follow the path round to the right and then go over a stile. Continue along the path to cross another stile onto the busy Dipton Mill road. From here turn left, and walk the short distance back to the start.

Notes

1. Dotland Park is a very interesting house that used to belong to the Priors

of Hexham Abbey in years gone by and was used by them as a hunting lodge. Some ecclesiastical architectural details dating from the 14th and 15th centuries can be seen externally, but the private interior hides far more.

2. Ahead and slightly right you will be able to see Black Hall. Straight ahead in the middle distance is Dukesfield, with Slaley forest beyond. Rotating towards the left you will see the hamlet of Juniper in the valley slope before you.

3. Mollersteads is said to be named after the mallow plants, which grew here in profusion in days gone by. These were collected and used to make dyes for the tanning industry in Hexham. The mallows were taken to the near-by hamlet of Dye House, where

Ecclesiastical window detail

they were processed to remove the dye. For more information on the history of the tanning industry in Hexham see Walk 15.

4. This is one of several old bridges in the district that appears to have had its inscribed name obliterated. Local folk think that this was done during the war at the time when, because invasion was threatened, all road signs were removed.

Walk 22: Dukesfield

Route: Lee Grange cross-road, Pethfoot Bridge, Middle Dukesfield, Fell Plantation, Viewley, Redlead Mill, Dukesfield Smelt Mill, Steel, Blackhall Mill, Juniper, Lee Grange.

Distance: 11km, 7 miles

High point: 254m

Ascent: 140m

Terrain: Woodland, riverside, lanes apart from one tricky stile. 🐕

Refreshments: Travellers Rest on the Hexham to Slaley road (B6306) near the junction with the Whitley Chapel road. Also Dipton Mill Inn nearer to Hexham, and The Rose and Crown in Slaley.

Map: OS Explorer OL43

The walk starts at the Lee Grange cross-road near Juniper, which is about 5km south of Hexham at grid ref. NY943589. Park on one of the grass verges and, at the cross-road, walk south-east down the un-marked cul-de-sac, where you will soon see Rowley Burn in the ra-vine on your right. At the valley bottom cross Pethfoot Bridge over Devil's Water and turn immediately right to follow the path through the trees, along the riverside. Cross the footbridge over Heron's Burn close to where it joins Devil's Water and follow the path up throuihg Folly Plantation to where it ends at a road. Cross the stile and turn left. After a short distance, take the right fork, signed to Dukesfield.

Walk for about half a kilometre to Middle Dukesfield . After about another half kilometre, turn right at the bend, following the Public Footpath way-marker into Slaley forest.

> As you walk along through the plantation you have good views to your right of Hexhamshire. Notice the huge anthills along the path. They are made of pine needles, and are hives of activity when the weather is warm.

At the gate, turn right and walk down the stony and then sandy path until you reach a lane by Viewley. Continue downhill on the metalled

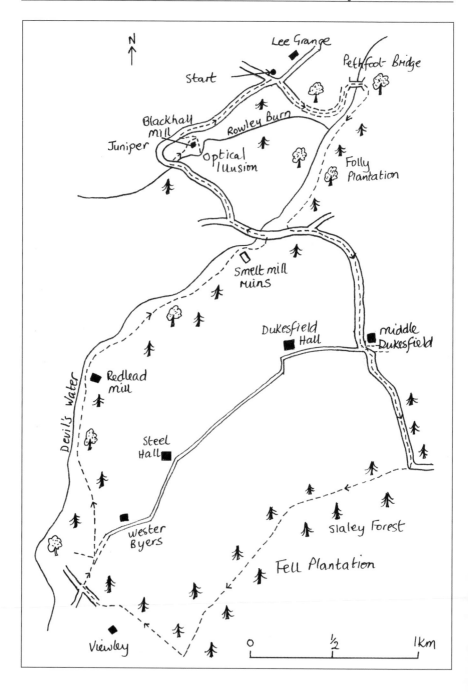

The remains of Dukesfield Smelt Mill

lane to where a footpath meets the lane and turn right, through a gate, way-marked as a Public Bridleway. Where the path forks, bear left, ignoring the smaller path leading straight down on your left. Continue downhill, keeping the conifers on your left in the direction of the river and cross the stile at Redlead Mill. Follow the cottage track and go through a gate, keeping the Devil's Water on your left.

In late autumn this area of forest has a rich variety of fungi.

Where the forest thins out on the right, an amazing gothic-styled ruin comes into view, which is all that remains of the old Dukesfield Smelt Mill (see Notes, 1). Continue along the path, go through the gate and turn left onto the road. Walk up to the first turn on the right, signed to Hexham. Take this road until it crosses the bridge over the Rowley Burn at Dye House. Immediately after the bridge, turn right, following the way-marker to Blackhall Mill. Go

Fly agaric – found in the woods

through the gate and walk diagonally left across the field to pass through the gap in the wall at the top corner. Walk behind a house, which was originally the corn mill, and emerge on the gravel path in the tiny hamlet of Blackhall Mill. If you make a short diversion from your path here, by turning right, you will come to the edge of the Rowley Burn, where there is an interesting outcrop of rock on the opposite bank (see Notes, 2). Retrace your footsteps to the old mill and then continue up the steep bank ahead. At the road, turn right and walk along the road through Juniper to return to your starting point just beyond this hamlet.

Notes

1. Dukesfield was the most important of the local smelt mills. The lead mined in Allendale had a high silver content, and the smelters here were known to be highly skilled and the best paid in the area. All that remains of the mill today are the two pointed arches of a bridge-like structure, which carried the flues from the mill to its chimneys. The mill was almost entirely demolished when work ceased here in 1836.

   Smelting was a highly skilled job. The ore from each vein was stored separately in the smelt mill and ore from the same vein was sent periodically to different mills to test the skill and care of individual smelters. Smelting was a seasonal job as winter passage over the lead routes made transportation impossible and fuel stocks of peat would be frozen. Smelters were then employed on drainage, hedging etc. For more information on the lead industry see Walks 25 and 4.

2. At this point of the Rowley Burn there is an outcrop of rock known as an igneous intrusion from the carboniferous period, the strata of which create the optical illusion of making the river appear to be flowing uphill.

Walk 23: Shildon Lead Mine

Route: Blanchland, Baybridge, Coat House, Pennypie House, Pennypie Fell, Shildon, Blanchland.

Distance: 7km, 4½ miles

High point: 385m

Ascent: 198m

Terrain: riverbank, fields, common moorland, just one tricky stile. 🐕

Refreshments: The Lord Crewe Arms, The White Monk Tea Rooms, Blanchland

Map: OS Explorer OL43

Begin the walk from the car park at the north edge of Blanchland, grid ref NY964504. Turn right from the car park and, at the cross roads, go straight ahead under the arch, through the village, and over the bridge which crosses the River Derwent (see Notes, 1). Immediately after the bridge turn right, through a gate, and walk up the grassy path through the trees. Pass through a gap in the fence, and into a larch wood. Soon you will pass a waterfall on the left. Continue to follow the path for about 1km, after which you will come to a gate leading to the road at Baybridge (see Notes, 2).

Turn right and walk over the bridge, continuing along the Blanchland road until you come to a way-marker on the left to Shildon. Go over a stile and walk up the sunken path ahead. Continue along this grassy path, to slowly ascend the hill. As you get towards the top, it is well worth a glance back to the sweeping Derwent valley and Baybridge.

> This is a blind valley, known locally as a 'hope'. This word forms part of the name of many villages and houses in the area, e.g. Stanhope, Killhope.

Continue straight on to a gate adjacent to a stile to give access to the next field. Walk diagonally across this field to pass through a kissing gate, next to a farm gate. Go through this gate, turning left onto the

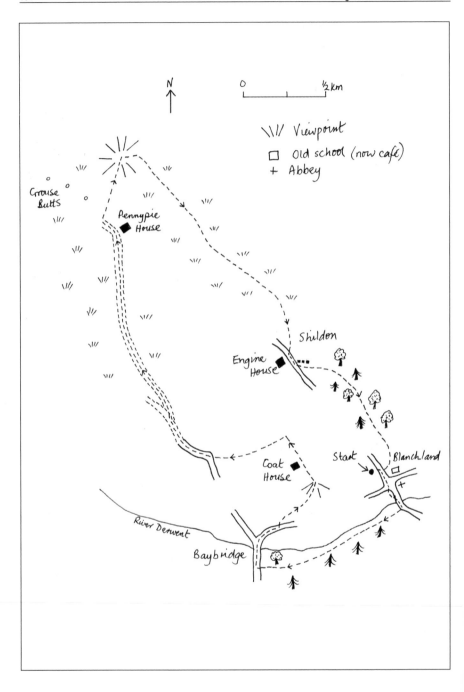

Blanchland Village

path, and walk up towards Coat House Farm. Pass the farm house on your left, and go through two gates onto a grassy track between stone walls. At the top of the track are three gates and you should go through the one on the left. Continue to the next gate, and then on along the top edge of the field. As you walk along, passing through two more gates, you will have continuing views on your left, of the Derwent valley and beyond. When you arrive at the lane, turn right and climb steeply uphill until you reach the fell gate. Shortly after going through the gate, leave the main track, and take the moorland track on your right. Follow this old drovers' track for about 1km, passing through another gate as you go. Eventually you will arrive at Pennypie House (see Notes, 3).

From here, follow the way-marker towards Ladycross, uphill along a stony path, which curves to the right and then goes up to a gate. After passing through the gate, branch immediately to the right.

From this point, on a clear day you will have a magnificent view to the east as far as Newcastle where two white tower blocks are visible just below the horizon. To the left are grouse butts, and diagonally left is a capped disused lead-mine shaft. The distant view behind you is of Bolti's Law (hill), and to its right is Killhope Law at 2200ft. (see Notes, 4).

Keep parallel to the wall on your right for a short distance and then go over a wall stile on the right. Follow the path diagonally left across the field towards a way-marker post ahead. Cross the wire fence at the stile. From here you make a gentle descent of Pennypie Fell, following the way-markers in a more or less straight line, all the way down until you cross a ladder stile over a wall and then a final stile in the tiny hamlet of Shildon (see Notes, 5).

From here turn left, and follow the path way-marked to Blanchland, that leads in front of two cottages. At the third cottage, go through a gate on the right. Bear left in front of the cottage to go through a gate in front of you. Walk ahead to the next gate, and into the wood. After the gate, turn sharp right to join the forest drive, where you turn left. Follow the drive until you reach a slip-track, going down on the right. This will bring you eventually to the rear of some cottages (see Notes, 6) and then out onto the Pennypie lane opposite the Blanchland car park.

Notes

1. The picturesque village of Blanchland is well worth a visit in its own right. The central buildings of golden sandstone, including the Lord Crewe Arms and the Abbey, have changed little in centuries, and information on their history is readily available in the village. Several of the Catherine Cookson stories that have been adapted for television, as well as other films and productions, have been filmed at Blanchland, with a mock market-place set up in the centre to represent Hexham in times gone by.

2. There is a picnic area and parking place at Baybridge, which you could use as an alternative to Blanchland. Baybridge had quite a reputation in the lead-mining days, as a lively community, prone to partying! A hundred years on, the hamlet has returned to tranquillity.

3. The word Pennypie is a corruption of 'penny pay', as this is where a toll of a penny was collected from drovers using the ancient track.

4. Grouse shooting is big business in this area and these lands are owned by the Crewe estate, as they have been for centuries. Each butt houses one

gun and provides shelter and sight cover as the birds approach. The area viewed across to Kilhope Law and Bolti's Law was a vast lead-mining area during the 17th, 18th and 19th centuries, and there are hidden shafts and ruined buildings all across the landscape, most of which remain unnoticed unless you search them out on an Ordnance Survey map.

5. There was a lead mine here at Shildon, and the impressive remains of the engine house and chimney can be seen opposite the stile. The building is currently listed by Northumberland as being in urgent need of repair and conservation. The cottages opposite the mine buildings were the homes of miners, rented to them by the mine owner. Miners were paid twice yearly, with a subsistence allowance (lent money) paid in between. This 'sub' plus charges for candles, gunpowder etc were deducted from the miner's pay, and if he had had a bad spell, he could frequently end up owing the company money. For more notes on lead mining see Walk 25 and Walk 2.

6. As you descend into Blanchland at the end of the walk you will pass behind some houses where a small television receiver can be seen. This serves the houses of Blanchland, as the use of television aerials on houses is banned as they would detract from the beauty of the old village. This is perhaps another reason why this location is so favoured by film and television producers of period drama.

Walk 24: Wagtail and Nookton

Route: Baybridge, Bale Hill, Deborah Plantation, Townfield, Wagtail, Hunstanworth, Baybridge.

Distance: 7km, 4½ miles

High point: 387m

Ascent: 176m

Terrain: woodland, fields, one steep climb.

Refreshments: Lord Crewe Arms and The White Monk Tea Rooms, Blanchland.

Map: OS Pathfinder Sheet 570

This walk starts in the car park in Baybridge, about half a mile west of Blanchland at Grid ref. NY958499. Walk out of the car park and turn right, cross the bridge over the River Derwent and start to walk up Bale Hill. This is a steep climb, so take your time. When you come to a way-marked gate on the right, enter Deborah Plantation and follow the track through the woods. Keep to the main track, which works its way down to go alongside Bolt's Burn. The track crosses the burn and then narrows down to a path, which becomes obscure. Stay close to the burn until you can cross it with care and walk along until you reach a footbridge (see Notes, 1).

> This damp area of ruins and old woodland has an abundance of mosses and lichens.

Cross the footbridge on your right and climb the steps ahead. Continue up the bank to cross a stile. Walk up the field with the wall on your right, go through a gate and continue up to the next gate.

> As you walk along this field, take time to look back at the hillside on the other side of the valley. The building with the chimney is the engine house of the Derwent Lead Mine at Ramshaw.

Go through the next gate and then walk straight across the field ahead towards the buildings of Townfield. Go through the gate and notice the old school and school house on your right. Cross the road and go

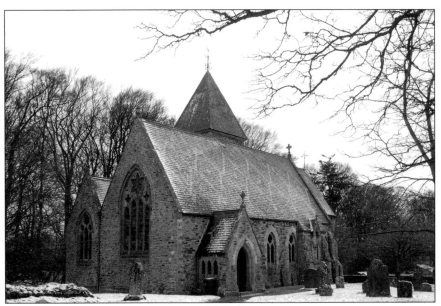

Hunstanworth Church

through the kissing gate following the way-marker straight ahead. As you ascend the field, look for the stile ahead.

At this point, look to your right for a view of Hunstanworth Church with its interesting Burgundian-styled roof, showing patterned light and dark slates. Look back for views of the lead mine at Ramshaw and Derwent Reservoir in the distance.

Cross the stile ahead and continue into the woods. Follow the path through the edge of the wood and leave by the stile over a wall. Bear diagonally right, towards a stile on the far wall, close to the overhead electricity cables. Either cross this rather difficult stile, or walk down the field a little way and go through a farm gate instead. Return to the path, which is quite well defined at this point, and walk to the next stile over a fence. Continue to, and go over, the next wall stile and walk ahead with the fence to your right. When you become level with Wagtail farm on your right, bear right, following the yellow arrows over another stile towards the farm. Go through the gate onto the lane and turn right. Walk along the lane and pass Cross Hill farm on your left, ignoring the footpath way-marker by the farm. Continue to the

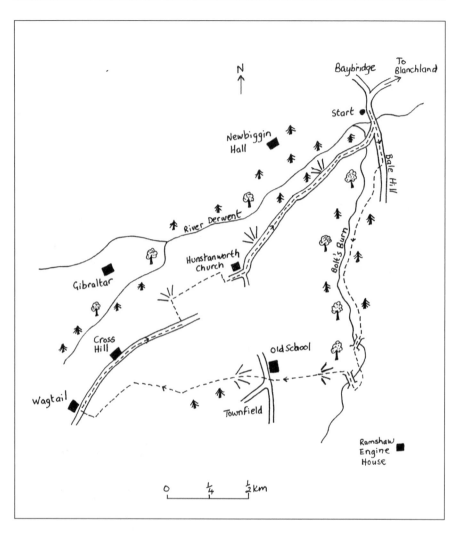

next way-marker on the left and go through the gate. Walk along the field with the wall on your left, cross a stile and turn right.

As you walk along with the wall on your right, look to the left and back a little way and you will see the ruin of Gibraltar, standing on its little spur of land between two rivers. As you approach the gate ahead, take time to look at the dry stone wall on your left. You can clearly see the line of through stones or thruffs at about half a metre up and again about another half metre up. These thruffs steady the wall and a country saying is that the bottom layer should jut out far enough for a rabbit to run along, and the top layer for a mouse to run along!

Continue through the gate ahead, edging the trees on your left. Go through the next gate and follow the wall on your right until you reach a stile where you turn right into the hamlet of Hunstanworth. Follow the lane round past the Church of St James (see Notes, 2).

At the T-junction turn left and follow the road back to Baybridge.

As you walk along this quiet road you will have picturesque views to the left of the steep, flat-bottomed Derwent Valley, with Nookton Wood on the far side. Then look out for Newbiggin Hall nestled in the trees (see Notes, 3). The autumn colours here are stunning.

At the T-junction turn left and return to the car park.

Notes

1. Parts of the culvert have caved in so you can see the structure. This whole area was heavily industrialised up to a century ago with many quarries and the shafts of Derwent Lead Mines. A little further on in the walk you will be able to look back at the Ramshaw engine house and chimney which still remain on the hillside although the lead mine finally closed towards the end of the 19th century. This building is a scheduled ancient monument and can be seen at close hand from a footpath off Bale Hill. When the lead industry was in full swing, the population of the Hunstanworth area had risen from 215 in 1801 to 778 in 1861. It was a similar story in all the nearby villages including Townfield and Ramshaw.

2. The present church was built on the site of a much earlier one in 1862. It was designed by Samuel Saunders Teulon, as was all the re-building of Hunstanworth in the boom time of lead mining. The re-building was the

Shaggy ink-cap

master plan of the Reverend Daniel Capper of nearby Newbiggin Hall. The Church is in the Early English style (apart from the decorated roof) with pitch pine furniture to the interior. Teulon designed several other buildings of note on both sides of the county boundary including a gatehouse to Newbiggin Hall and the school in Blanchland. The parish registers of Hunstanworth go back to 1659 at which time there was a pele tower adjacent to the church. Peles (fortified towers) are quite rare as far south as County Durham, but the fact that some exist is evidence that border raids sometimes did stretch this far south during the troubled 15th and 16th centuries. The remains of the pele can still be seen in the church-yard.

3. Newbiggin Hall was the family seat of Daniel Capper, at the time that he commissioned the re-building of Hunstanworth. Unfortunately Newbiggin Hall was destroyed by fire in 1904, but the house we see today was built in Neo-classical style in 1906.

Walk 25: Carriers' Way

Route: Hesleywell road end, Long Lee, Low Hope, Blackburn Head, Carriers Way, Burntshield Haugh, Hesleywell farm, road end.

Distance: 8.5km, 5¼ miles

High Point: 392m

Ascent: 267m

Terrain: common moorland, lanes.

Refreshments: Travellers Rest near Slaley on B6306, Dipton Mill Inn on the Hexham to Whitley Chapel road

Map: OS Explorer OL43

This route is very exposed, with few landmarks, and should not be attempted in poor visibility. As with all walks, it is strongly recommended that you carry the relevant OS map.

Begin the walk from the cattle grid on the road leading to Harwood Shield, grid ref. NY911525 where there is ample parking on the grass verge. Walk back a short distance to the road junction and turn right. Descend the hill towards Hesleywell, but take the first lane on the right. Walk down, passing Folly house, until you come to a gate, which opens onto another metalled lane on the left, leading to Long Lee farm. Enter the farmyard and bear right across the yard between the buildings, to two adjacent gates. Taking the right-hand gate, descend the field keeping close to the fence on your right. Cross the stile into a birch wood and descend the steps to the bridge over the Devil's Water (see Notes, 1).

Bearing slightly to the left, ascend the hill. You will soon see the buildings of the now disused Low Hope farm ahead to your left. After going through a gap in the stone wall on your left, head uphill to Low Hope. At the left end of the buildings, go through a gate, cross the yard and leave the old farm by a small gate. Out of the yard, bearing only slightly left you will pick up a rough stony track heading uphill in a southerly direction. This rough way eventually improves into a

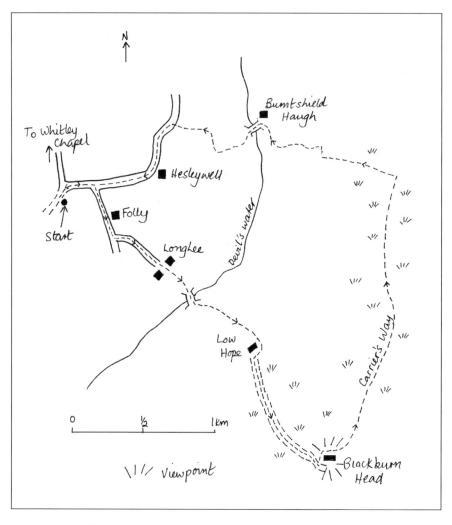

sandy Land Rover track which swings left to reach the shooting cabin
at Blackburn Head (see Notes, 2).

With the hut door behind you, pick up the track to the right which is
the Carriers' Way (see Notes, 3). Pass through a gate and continue on
around the hillside for about 2km. This path is way-marked in several
places and has one more gate for you to pass through before reaching
a cross-road with a marker post with several arrows on each side.

Burning off heather on the moor – storage hut in foreground

Here, take the narrower path to the left to descend the fell, following the way-marker posts all the way down to a dog-leg right then left near the bottom of the hill. Look at the lovely sheep pen as you pass, and continue the now stony track into Burntshieldhaugh farm.

This interestingly named farm was apparently built at a place of low ground with a burnt-out hut!

At the farm yard, pass through two gates to a bridge over the Devil's Water on your left. Follow the farm road out onto the metalled lane. Turn left on the lane and follow it up past Hesleywell farm. Continue uphill to return to your starting point.

Notes

1. The name Devil's Water is a corruption of the name d'Eiville. The Norman family of this name owned the land from the time of William the Conqueror.

2. The name Blackburn Head refers to the source of the burn running over the black land of heather moor. This is a good view point across Hexhamshire and along Devil's Water to the north and east, and in the

opposite direction over Hexhamshire Common towards Allenheads. These are some of the best grouse moors in the country, and in order to produce the required number of birds by August 12th each year, the moors must be skilfully managed. Each spring large tracts of the old heather are burnt off to ground level to allow the growth of new shoots which provide the food for young chicks.

3. Part of this walk joins one of the old tracks known as Carriers Way. As described in other walks, the lead mining industry formed a large part of life in this region in the 17th, 18th and 19th centuries. The lead ore was transported to the smelt mills at Dukesfield, Langley and Allendale along these tracks, several of which still wend their way over the moors today. The lead produced at the smelt mills was carried by the ponies to Hexham and then on to Newcastle for further distribution. The ore and lead were transported on trains of pack horses. 20-50 Galloway ponies would carry a Newcastle Fother, i.e. just over one ton of lead. For more information on the lead industry see Walk 22.

Walk 26: Glacial Meltwater Channel

Route: Harwood Shield, Riddlehamhope, Beldon End Plantation, Carriers Way, Harwood Shield.

Distance: 7km, 4½ miles

High point: 407m

Ascent: 213m

Terrain: moorland, forest. Only one stile that may be tricky for large dogs, near the end. 🐕

Refreshments: Travellers Rest near Slaley on B6306, Dipton Mill Inn on the Hexham to Whitley Chapel road

Map: OS Explorer OL43

To make a longer walk, this one can be combined with Walk 27 – Halleywell – as they both have the same starting point but cover different and varied countryside. The combined walk is about 11.5km or 8 miles.

To get to the start of this walk, take the road south from Whitley Chapel for about 6km in the direction of Harwood Shield Farm, where the road runs out. There is room to park on the grass verge just before the farm gate at grid ref NY906513. Please do not block the gate or farm road.

Walk through the farm and continue straight ahead along the path, crossing a bridge with an inscribed stone (see Notes, 1).

> Walking on for the next 1.5km or so you should see red grouse, golden plover and other moorland birds which nest extensively in the heather. For more information on grouse management see Walk 25.

Where the track bears right to Heatheryburn, go straight on to pass through a gate ahead. Follow the track which curves left to give a view of Beldon Burn in the valley ahead. Go through the gate and pass the ruin of Riddlehamhope, which was formerly a shooting lodge (see Notes, 2). Continue through two gates and along a grassy track. After

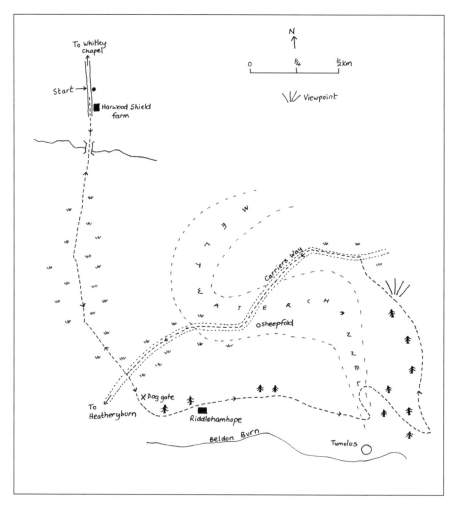

passing over a ladder stile you will see a circle of trees ahead surrounded by a wall.

These trees mark the position of an ancient tumulus.

Follow the path left and then right and cross a glacial melt-water channel, more of which will be seen later in the walk. Go over another stile and then ascend the hillside through the mixed conifer woodland. At the next gate turn left onto a grassy track, following the line of trees on your left.

Ruin of Riddlehamhope Hunting Lodge

At the top of this hill you will have an extensive view of Hexhamshire ahead.

Where the trees end, take a moment to look to the left in the near distance to see more of the shaping of the landscape by the glacial meltwater channel (see Notes, 3). Walk straight ahead, until you meet the hollow track through the heather which is the Carriers Way (see Notes, 4). Turn left and follow this path around some of the glacial channel on your left and continue as the path descends diagonally into the channel.

Notice the circular sheep fold on the left.

Continue to a stile on the left and then follow the board-walk across the marshy land. Ascend the slope bearing right and continue along the Carriers Way until you reach the final stile onto the main track. (People with large dogs may need to divert left here. Walk to a gate in front of the plantation to gain access to the track). Turn right and walk about 1.5km back to Harwood Shield Farm.

Notes

1. The inscription on this bridge appears to read 'Private Bridge'.

2. A manor house is recorded as having existed at Riddlehamhope as early as 1214. The building that remains today was in use until about 1950 as a hunting lodge and has fallen into disrepair since then. Hilary Kristensen, in her book 'Memories of Hexhamshire' (Wagtail Books 1999), shows a photograph of the Duchess of Connaught at Riddlehamhope together with her gamekeeper in 1924. To the far west of the outbuildings are the remains of what is thought to have been a 16th-century bastle, or fortified house, with walls over 1m thick.

3. Much of the Northumberland landscape was shaped by glacial action during the last ice-age. The meltwater from a glacier can wear channels beneath the glacier or along and in front of the advancing ice. Major meltwater channels such as this one can appear to be out of place in the landscape and exceptionally large relative to the water running through them (if any). Also, because the water which formed this channel was under the heavy pressure of ice, it may be at odds with the normal surrounding drainage channels.

4. Carriers' ways and drovers' tracks criss-cross the Northumberland countryside and are reminders of the transport systems of its industrial past. Coal and lead were the main products carried long distances by pony trains before the advent of the railways. For more information on the Carriers Way see Walk 25.

Walk 27: Halleywell

Route: Harwood Shield, Carriers Way, Riddlehamhope Fell, Halleywell, Beldon Burn, Heatheryburn, Harwood Shield.

Distance: 7.5km, 4¾ miles

High point: 456m

Ascent: 202m

Terrain: Moorland, tracks.

Refreshments: Travellers Rest near Slaley on B6306, Dipton Mill Inn on the Hexham to Whitley Chapel road

Map: OS Explorer OL43

This is an ideal walk for a summer evening with the curlews calling across the moor and the western sky opening up before you for a glorious sunset. Alternatively, if you would like a longer daytime walk, this one can be combined with Walk 26 as they both have the same starting point but take you through different and varied countryside. The combined walk is about 11.5km or 8 miles.

To get to the start of this walk, take the road south from Whitley Chapel for about 6km in the direction of Harwood Shield Farm, where the road runs out. There is room to park on the grass verge just before the farm gate at grid ref NY906513. Please do not block any gates.

Walk through the farm and continue straight ahead along the path, crossing a bridge with an inscribed stone (see Walk 26 for notes on this bridge).

Walking on for the next 1.5km or so you should see red grouse and other

Curlew in flight

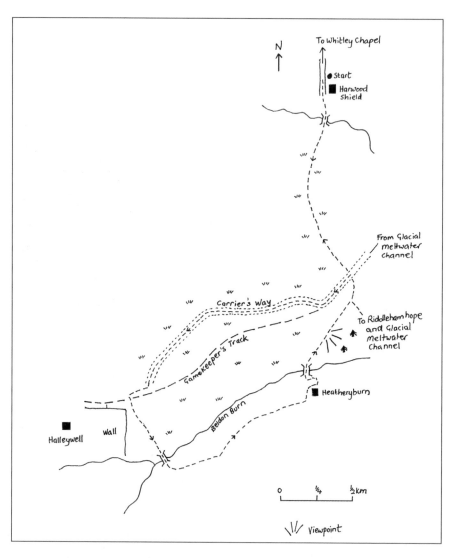

To Whitley Chapel

N

● Start

■ Harwood Shield

From Glacial meltwater channel

To Riddlehamhope and Glacial meltwater channel

Carrier's Way

Gamekeeper's Track

■ Heatheryburn

■ Halleywell

Wall

Beldon Burn

0   ¼   ½ km

\│/ Viewpoint

moorland birds which nest extensively in the heather. For more information on grouse management see Walk 25.

When you reach a stile on the left, turn right onto the track which is part of the Carriers' Way (see Walks 26 and 25 for more information on the Carriers' Way). Follow the track making a gentle ascent of Riddlehamhope Fell for about 2km.

Moorland by Halleywell

On the tops there is a lichen paradise with variously coloured species forming random patterns along the heather margins (see Notes, 1).

Where the path eventually peters out you will see the gravelled game-keepers' track to your left (see Notes, 2). Turn right onto this track and walk for a short distance until you reach the wall on the left.

Ahead is the entrance to the ruined house Halleywell, though it is not visible at this point. It has not been occupied since the 1950s, and the structure may not be safe, but you can explore the outside if you like. But return to this spot before commencing the walk as the way through the Halleywell fields is marshy and difficult.

Turn left just before the wall and follow the wall down for a while before cutting diagonally left across the field, working your way to the footbridge across the Beldon Burn. Having crossed the bridge, bear left, following the grassy path up over the hill and on to another path where you turn left. Walk ahead and cross a small stream, continuing up and along the grassy path through four gates, finally descending to Heatheryburn farm. Skirt around the left side of the farm buildings and go through a gate onto the farm track. Turn left and walk down the farm track to cross the burn at the bridge. Go over a cattle grid and then ascend the track, taking time to look down on the Beldon Burn on your right. Eventually you turn left to rejoin the main Harwood Shield path, and walk the final 1.5km to your starting point.

Notes

1. This Hexhamshire moor is part of the Pennine chain and consists mainly of limestone covered with poorly drained blanket peat. The peat was formed 6,000-7,000 years ago from the typical vegetation of heather, cotton grass and sphagnum moss. The dominant grasses are Bent and Sheep's Fescue. Rowan, hazel, birch and alder grow in sporadic clumps in cleughs (ravines).

2. This area forms part of the best grouse moors in England and grouse shooting is big business. See Notes for Walk 25. You will also pass piles of grit in the heather, placed there by the gamekeepers to aid the digestion of heather by the birds.

Walk 28: Best View in Hexhamshire

Route: Kingslaw Plantation, Moss Hill, Rowley Wood, Crabtree Ford, Long Drag, Kingslaw Plantation.

Distance: 9.5km, 6¼ miles

High point: 338m

Ascent: 218m

Terrain: moorland, rough track, lane.

Refreshments: Travellers Rest near Slaley on B6306, Dipton Mill Inn on the Hexham to Whitley Chapel road

Map: OS Explorer OL43

Winter or summer, do this walk on a bright day as the views are panoramic and stunning. Drive south from Whitley Chapel past the Church gate towards Harwood Shield. After about two miles, at Whitehall Methodist Chapel, take the right fork to Westburnhope. Continue up this lane and park at the bend on the far side of the cattle grid at grid ref NY903544.

Walk along the lane ahead in a north-westerly direction, keeping the plantation to your right. Where the trees end, walk on a few more metres to the Millennium bench, placed there by local people, and drink in The Best View in the Shire! On a clear day you will be able to see as far as the high-rise flats in Newcastle. Properly refreshed, continue along the lane, over a cattle grid and on for about 2km to cross Rowley Burn.

> Notice the inscription on Westburnhope Bridge. This is one of several old bridges in the district that appears to have had its inscribed name obliterated. Local folk think that this was done during the war at the time when, because invasion was threatened, all road signs were removed.

Pass Westburnhope farm drive on your left and go through the gate in front of you. Climb the rutted track uphill, taking your time as this is

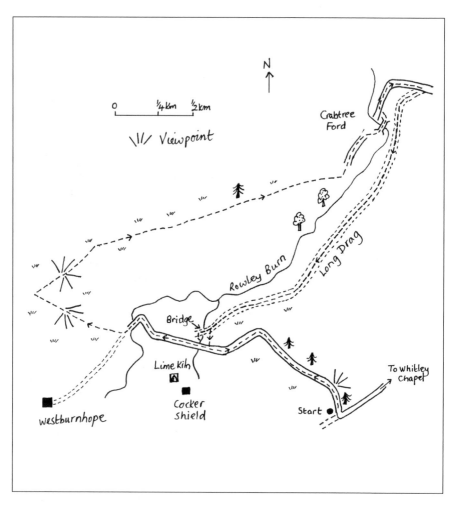

steep. Pause and turn to admire the views behind you (see Notes, 1). Continue uphill through two gates until you reach the open moor.

> Lapwings, golden plover, curlews and black grouse all nest on these moors as well as red grouse. You may even be lucky enough to spot a Hen Harrier or Kite sweeping lazily in a low arc above the ground.

Turn right, and keeping the stone wall on your right, follow the narrow track for about 1.5km to a gate. Go through the gate onto a stony track at Burntridge Plantation. Continue along the track for

Entrance to The Drag

another 1km and cross the footbridge at Crabtree Ford. Walk uphill on the lane, and after the bend, enter the first gate set back a little on your right. This takes you onto a wide track known as The Long Drag (see Notes, 2). Follow The Drag for about 2km, going through one gate.

Take time to admire the views of the steep gorge of the Rowley Burn on your right.

Just before you reach the second gate, you will notice that you are standing on a little road bridge over a small gully. You may like to climb down the hillside to your left and see the wonderful arched stonework and cobbled floor going under the road. Back on The Drag, just before this bridge, turn left onto a narrow path and head uphill towards a small gate in the wall. Go through the gate and turn left onto the lane. This is the lane you started on, and by following it uphill you will have the pleasure of a second sighting of the Best View in the Shire before returning to your car.

Notes

1. If you turn round at this point and look across to the hillside behind you, you should be able to make out the structure that resembles a tunnel entrance. This is an individual lime kiln, used in the past by farmers to produce lime from limestone. Although the underlying rock is mainly limestone, the topsoil tends to be acidic, hence the spreading of lime to neutralise the soil. For more information on lime kilns see Walk 1.

2. The Long Drag is not a public footpath, but with kind permission from the local farmer, the public are permitted to walk this section, except for the very last bit, where we make a diversion. It is named after the journeys made in the past by the grouse shooters on ponies being 'dragged' up to Lord Allendale's grouse moors. These days they come in Land Rovers.

Bibliography

Archer, David (1992) *Land of Singing Waters*. Spredden Press

Bellamy, David and Quayle, Brendan (1992) *England's Last Wilderness*. Boxtree

Bowden, Charles (2001) *The Last Horsemen*. Granada

Dixon, Hubert (1974) *An Allendale Miscellany*. Graham

Fraser, George MacDonald (1979) *The Steel Bonnets*. Pan

Gibson, Wilfred Wilson (2003) *Homecoming*. Wagtail Press

Graham, Frank (1978) *Tynedale from Blanchland to Carter Bar*. Graham

Harley, Susan (1999) *In the Bewick Vein*. Honeycrook Press

Hunt, C. J. (1984) *The Lead Miners of the Northern Pennines*. Davis and Kelsall

Kristensen, Hilary (2000) *Memories of Hexhamshire*. Wagtail Books

Lomas, Richard (1996) *County of Conflict*. Tuckwell Press

Lunn, Angus (2004) *Northumberland with Alston Moor*. Collins

Pevsner, Nikolaus (1992) *The Buildings of Northumberland*. Penguin Books

Robertson, Alastair (1999) *Lime Kilns of the North Pennines*. North Pennines Heritage Trust

Ryder, Peter (1996) *Bastle Houses in the North Pennines*. North Pennines Heritage Trust

Sopwith, Robert (1994) *Thomas Sopwith Surveyor*. Pentland Press

Tomlinson, W.W. (1968) *Tomlinson's Comprehensive Guide to Northumberland*. David & Charles

Turnbull, Les (1975) *The History of Lead Mining*. Harold Hill

Wainwright, Alfred (1992) *On the Pennine Way*. Mermaid Books

Walker, Kevin (1990) *The Complete Walker*. Ashford

Watson, Godfrey (1970) *'Goodwife Hot and Other Places'* Sandhill Press

Watson, Godfrey (1985) *The Border Reivers*. Sandhill Press

Wright, Geoffrey (1989) *The Northumbrian Uplands*. David & Charles

Also of Interest:

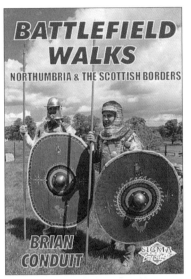

BATTLEFIELD WALKS: NORTHUMBRIA & THE SCOTTISH BORDERS

Brian Conduit

Historian, experienced walker and author, Brian Conduit, has produced a collection of walks describing 22 military engagements covering all the main battlefield sites in the area. The grandest military monument in the whole of Britain, Hadrian's Wall, is visited and the walks also feature such military events as: the Viking raid on Lindisfarne in 793; sieges of the two greatest border strongholds, Carlisle and Berwick-on-Tweed; the fates of abbeys on both sides of the border caught up in the incessant warfare; the surprise attack by the German navy on the east coast of England at the start of World War I. £7.95

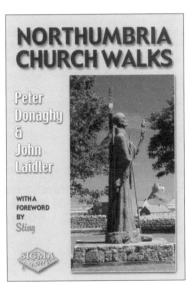

NORTHUMBRIA CHURCH WALKS

Peter Donaghy & John Laidler

With a Foreword by Sting

International rock star Sting recalls how he has often found solutions to life's problems while walking in Northumbria on "long solitary walks to encounter solitude and inspiration." These 30 circular walks are from 4 to 12 miles with alternative shorter options, each combined with over 40 churches open to visitors. Insight is provided into our cultural and artistic heritage with fine examples of stained glass windows, ancient crosses, medieval fonts, wood carvings and sculptures old and new. £8.95

NORTHUMBRIA WALKS WITH CHILDREN

Stephen Rickerby

Sigma publish a range of 'Walks with Children' for several of the most attractive parts of England. This book includes 20 walks, suitable for families, covering the North East from the Tees to the Tweed. 'This is a splendid collection that will excite and stimulate youngsters.' – *Sunderland Echo*
£6.95

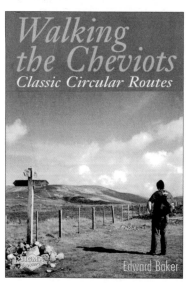

WALKING THE CHEVIOTS:
Classic Circular Routes

Edward Baker

This well-established book is one of the few guides to a true wilderness area, written by an author who has lived in the Cheviots all his life. Nearly 50 walks, from 2 to 14 miles. "A must for the Cheviot walker, whether experienced in the area or a visitor eager to explore this unique range of northern hills." – *Rambling Today*
£8.95

All of our books are available through booksellers. In case of difficulty, or for a free catalogue, please contact: **SIGMA LEISURE, STOBART HOUSE, PONTYCLERC, PENYBANC ROAD, AMMANFORD, CARMS SA18 3HP**

Phone: 01269 593100 Fax: 01269 596116
info@sigmapress.co.uk
Full details of all of our books can be found at our Web site: www.sigmapress.co.uk